Foreign Seizures

SABBATINO AND THE ACT OF STATE DOCTRINE

by
Eugene F. Mooney

A UNIVERSITY OF
KENTUCKY STUDY

UNIVERSITY OF KENTUCKY PRESS

CONTENTS

INTRODUCTION

They're rioting in Africa;
They're starving in Spain.
There are hurricanes in Florida
And Texas needs rain.

The whole world is festering
With unhappy souls.
The French hate the Germans
The Germans hate the Poles.
Italians hate Yugoslavs,
South Africans hate the Dutch;
And I don't like anybody very much.*

* These lines are from a little ditty recorded a few years ago by the Kingston Trio called "The Merry Minuet" which, they facetiously claimed, was scheduled for an album to be entitled "The Kingston Trio Plays John Foster Dulles."

$\mathcal{J}$HE AMERICAN and French revolutions of the late 1700s are familiar historical events, but modern revolutions are equally familiar. Within the lifetime of any man under fifty years of age the world has been plagued by wars and almost continual civil strife. These political events have been invariably attended by seizures of private property by various nations. Even the following partial list of these transactions is impressive:

Country	Date	Property Seized
Russia	1917	practically the entire economy
Bolivia	1936	oil, tin mines
Mexico	1938	oil, land
Turkey	1938	cement and other industries
Estonia ⎫ Latvia ⎬ Lithuania ⎭	1940	banks, transport, mines, other industry
Bulgaria	1942, 1947	banks, industry in general
France	1944-1945	coal, Banque de France, airlines, electricity, gas, two-thirds of insurance, Renault
Holland	1945	mining
Czechoslovakia	1945	mining, food, banking, insurance—involving 65 percent of industrial capacity
Hungary	1945-1946	industry, transport, coal, electricity, carbide, food, power, oil, banks
Poland	1946	17 branches of the economy (including brewing, textiles, printing, mines, oil utilities, iron, steel, sugar)
Austria	1946-1947	credit institutions, coal, iron/steel, oil, some engineering, power and transport—involving 22 percent of all industrial workers
Britain	1947	coal, transport, electricity, steel

Country	Date	Property Seized
Roumania	1947-1948	banks, mines, insurance, transport
Burma	1948	land, forestry, river transport, oil
New Zealand	1949	coal
China	1950	most private business and commerce
Iran	1951	oil
Bolivia	1952	oil, tin mines
Guatemala	1953	land
India	1955	Imperial Bank of India
Yugoslavia	1956	42 branches of the economy (including mines, oil, banks, insurance, wholesaling)
Egypt	1956	Universal Suez Maritime Canal Co.
Indonesia	1957	Dutch properties
Iraq	1957	transport, electricity, food, textiles
Cuba	1959-1960	oil refineries, American businesses, land
Brazil	1959-1960	some public utilities

Most nationalizations have occurred in the context of the on-going global process of organizing the territory of the earth into nation states. Since World War II this process has taken the form of a movement into independent nation states. Seizures of alien-owned property have thus been motivated largely by the same sociopolitical forces of nationalism driving the basic organization process. One of the unfortunate elements of nationalism is the fear of foreign economic domination. Normally the underdeveloped nations are most fearful of foreign economic domination; yet one of the most cogent statements of the Yankee-go-home attitude comes from a modern industrial nation where more than 30 percent of the total fixed assets are American controlled:

Many Canadians are worried about such a large degree of economic decision-making being in the hands of non-residents or in the hands of Canadian companies controlled by non-residents. This concern has arisen because of the fact that most of it is centered in one country, the United States, and because most of it is in the form of equities which, in the ordinary course of events, are never likely to be repatriated . . . if a period of political or economic instability should occur they might develop into demands for restrictive or discriminatory action of an extreme kind.[1]

[1] U.N. Dep't of Economic and Social Affairs, "Foreign Private Investments in the Latin American Free-Trade Area," 14 (1961).

3

In light of this particular prospect, it is not surprising that less developed nations fear domination. There is, of course, a firm factual basis for these fears in many instances.[2]

The prospect of expropriation would not be quite so alarming if these takings normally were always fully compensated for by the host country. Such, unfortunately, is not the case. One writer has noted that "compensation is almost always promised and almost never paid,"[3] and the overall

[2] The oil industries of Mexico in the late 1930s and of Iran in the early 1950s were 100% foreign controlled, and nationalization in Eastern Europe following World War II occurred against a similar economic background. Foreign investments in Poland in 1939 were $19.6 million and constituted 32.7% of the total capital of Polish industry. The agricultural land nationalization in the 1920s by Czechoslovakia involved 24% of the total surface area of the state, of which 42.5% was owned by foreigners—about one-eighth of the entire State. The Roumanian nationalizations of 1948 included the 24% share of the nation's industry owned by foreigners. See Foighel, *infra* note 3. This is not merely historical data from a bygone age. Brazil nationalized several public utilities in 1959-1960 and the Brazilian envoy to Washington in March of 1963 gave notice that further nationalizations of foreign-owned assets were being contemplated. (There are at present in Brazil approximately $1.5 billion in American-owned assets to which these threats may apply.) Only the military coup in April 1964 forestalled these threatened takings. The New York *Times* for April 3, 1963, carried stories concerning military revolts in Argentina and Guatemala and a large-scale anti-American public demonstration in Brazil; the Canadian national elections held during the spring of 1963 were conducted amidst a thinly-veiled "hate America" campaign by the near-winner Diefenbaker.

[3] Foighel, "Nationalization—A Study in the Protection of Alien Property in International Law," 26 Nordisk Tidsskrift for International Fed. 89 (1956). There have been many American commentaries concerning this field of international law, some of which are: Dietz, "The Disregard for Property in International Law," 56 Nw. U. L. Rev. 87 (1961); Timberg, "Sovereign Immunity, State Trading, Socialism and Self-Deception," 56 Nw. U. L. Rev. 109 (1961); Thomas, "Protection of Property of Citizens Abroad," 1 Inst. on Private Investment Abroad 417 (S.W. Legal Found. 1959); and Bohan, "U.S. Public and Private Investments in Latin America," 4 Inst. on Private Investment Abroad and Foreign Trade 25 (S.W. Legal Found. 1962). Many nationalizations are initiated with no intention to compensate creditors or ex-owners and in which no hypocritical promises are made: the Soviets, for example, apparently never entertained the notion in 1917, although following World War II some effort apparently was made to compensate for seizures. The Suez Canal nationalization proceeded

picture throughout the past fifty years has grown increasingly gloomy for the private investor as he watches seizures being legally protected.

This gloom is in no way lightened by the decision of the United States Supreme Court in the famous *Sabbatino* case, which wound a tortuous way through the American courts.[4] The circumstances in that case and the focus of this study concern seizure of alien-owned private property by a governmental act[5] which violates the reasonable expectations of the people participating in our international economy. The United States Supreme Court decided that the courts of this country are required to defer to that governmental act, thereby lending it authority and to that extent aiding in the effecting of the seizure. Such a result follows from a doctrinaire and legalistic rule which the Court held was the law of the land.

The burden of this book is to demonstrate that this legalistic doctrine, when pushed beyond its proper purpose, becomes heretical and is utterly without justification in light of the realities of the past practice of our nation. Moreover, such extended versions of the doctrine embody no policy

---

with considerable candor on the premise that extraterritorially situated assets of the company will be used to pay off creditors and the ex-owners will get United Arab Republic state bonds payable from the profits.

[4] See Appendix I for a bibliography of scholarly commentary on the *Sabbatino* case during its three year passage through the federal courts and on the Hickenlooper Amendment to the Foreign Assistance Act of 1964.

[5] An "act of state" is simply a governmental act, or in the words of Judge Clark in Banco de España v. Federal Reserve Bank, 114 F.2d 438, 444 (CCA 2, 1940) "By a government act is meant no more than a step physically taken by persons capable of exercising the sovereign authority of a foreign nation." Another exposition defines it thus: "The expression 'act of state' usually denotes an executive or administrative exercise of sovereign power by an independent State or potentate, or by its duly authorized agents or officers. The expression, however, is not a term of art, and it obviously may and is often intended, to include legislative and judicial acts such as a statute, decree or order, or a judgment of a superior court." Mann, "The Sacrosanctity of the Foreign Act of State," 59 Law. Q. Rev. 42, 155 (1943).

which a nation committed to maintaining an international economy can accept dogmatically, and this application of it is indefensible in the light of its origin, the history of its past application, and the pressing current requirements of our international economy.

American courts have been responsible for this misapplication. Their decisions on foreign seizures of alien-owned property fall into three general groups. The South American seizures gave birth to the Act of State Doctrine in the highly specialized context of our hemispheric history. The Doctrine made sense at the time and under the circumstances surrounding its creation. Later when the Communist seizures occurred the Act of State Doctrine did not fit the various fact situations smoothly, although similar or analogous judicial dogma was often invoked. But the Communist seizure cases formed a major doctrinal line of authority concerning foreign seizures. The third major doctrinal line of case decisions arose from the Nazi seizures during World War II and culminated in the notorious Bernstein cases.

Prefacing herein a study of these three groups of judicial decisions is a look at the history of the Act of State Doctrine. The *Sabbatino* case and the Hickenlooper Amendment form a major pronouncement, and thus are the pivot point of this study. Thereafter, some of the troublesome complications of the Sabbatino ruling are explored. The study closes with a suggestion for some major parameters of a new judicial Act of State Doctrine.

6

1

GENESIS OF THE ACT
OF STATE DOCTRINE

$\mathcal{T}$HE ACT OF State Doctrine is said to have begun during the dawn of Anglo-American jurisprudence with *Blads Case* in 1674. The report of the facts in this case is a little confusing, and the judgment of the court was obviously colored somewhat by the domestic squabble between English law courts and chancery courts, which was still going on even at that date, but the Doctrine can be spelled out by a close reading of the opinion.

England and Denmark had executed a peace treaty which ostensibly permitted free trade among their citizens and territories. Bamfield, an English citizen who had for several years traded with natives of Iceland, a Danish territory, had his goods seized by one Blad acting under letters patent from the King of Denmark that purported to give him exclusive trading rights in Iceland. The seized goods were sentenced by a Danish chancellor in Iceland, execution was issued and served, and two-thirds of the value of the goods was paid over to the King of Denmark. Subsequently, Bamfield commenced a lawsuit in England against Blad asking for damages because of the latter's trespass committed in seizing Bamfield's goods in Iceland. Bamfield claimed that the peace treaty gave him a right to trade and that the Danish letters patent were therefore illegal. Blad thereupon brought an action in chancery asking a perpetual injunction against Bamfield prohibiting him from proceeding in the trespass lawsuit. Bamfield stubbornly insisted on his interpretation of the peace treaty. The learned chancellor granted the injunction upon the following reasoning:

But in truth this pretence of articles of peace must needs fail the Defendants; for the articles of free trade are reciprocal, and are understood on both sides, with exception to the laws and customs of each kingdom. Put the case then that a Danish ship should trade to the Barbadoes, or any other of his majesty's foreign plantations, and were thereupon taken and seized, or should break in upon the privileges granted by his majesty to the East India Company, and were there arrested at Bantam or Fort St. George, doubtless this were no breach of the treaty on our part; and if any of his majesty's subjects who seized that ship at the Barbadoes, or judges, should be then molested and prosecuted in Denmark, in a private action, for what they did in obedience to the laws of their king and country, it would look like such a breach on their part as might well occasion a further rupture on ours. . . . Now, after all this, to send it to a trial at law, where either the Court must pretend to judge of the validity of the king's letters patent in Denmark, or of the exposition and meaning of the articles of peace; or that a common jury should try whether the English have a right to trade in Iceland, is monstrous and absurd.[1]

Embodied in this ancient case are all the arguments which come subsequently to be involved in practically every Act of State case to arise during the next two hundred years:

[1] Blads case, 3 Swan's App. 603, 36 Eng. Rep. 991 (1674).

8

(1) personal immunity of officials for executing national law, (2) the possibility that a judicial inquiry would be a casus belli, (3) possible interference with executive conduct of foreign relations, (4) the incompetence of the judiciary to deal with matters involving foreign or international law, and (5) the Christian spirit to do unto others as you would have them do unto you.

The rather pretentious language of the Act of State Doctrine comes initially from the *Duke of Brunswick* case in 1848. His Serene Highness Charles Frederick William Augustus was the reigning Duke of Brunswick near Hanover, Germany, in 1830. He was also an English national and owned property in Brunswick, France, and England. That year, however, he became involved in or failed to put down a revolutionary movement in Brunswick which alarmed King William IV of Hanover, who was also an English subject. King William IV by decree issued in Germany thereupon appointed the Duke of Cambridge guardian of the Duke of Brunswick, thereby deposing him and seizing his property. The original Duke initially tried to regain his throne by peaceable individual protest, and then in 1843 he filed a bill in chancery in England against King William IV asking that the decree of 1830 be set aside and that an accounting be made, obtaining personal service on King William IV who was temporarily residing in England that year. King William IV demurred, asserting a want of jurisdiction because of his personal immunity as a sovereign and because the foreign decree was an act of state; the Duke, however, insisted it was just another lawsuit between Englishmen. The Rolls Court sustained the King's demurrer and dismissed the bill solely on the sovereign immunity point, but on appeal, the House of Lords broadened the basis in affirming the dismissal:

. . . [A] foreign Sovereign, coming into this country, cannot be made responsible here for an act done in his sovereign character in his own country; whether it be an act right or wrong, whether according to the Constitution of that country or not, the Courts of this country cannot sit in judgment upon the act of a Sovereign, effected by virtue of his sovereign authority. . . .[2]

Perhaps because of the heraldic quality of this language, the metaphor of "sitting in judgment" has been a fixture of the Doctrine for over one hundred years. This particular verbal formulation is not merely striking figurative language; it also embodies some of our deeper conceptualizations concerning the very nature of law itself.

Western legal philosophy postulates the necessity of sovereign nation states. International organization of the globe since the Middle Ages has been based upon the notion of the nation state and territorial law. The primary assumption of this idea is the exclusivity of a given sovereign's political authority within a certain territory, authority based upon a physical power which might or might not exist in fact. Thus the earth's surface is blanketed by a patchwork of municipal law. The physical exploration and basic political organization of the earth since the fall of the Holy Roman Empire has been largely implemented by the simplicity, orderliness, and efficiency of the concept of national sovereignty. The global checkerboard of autonomous nations is sustained today by this same mechanism which keeps all these separate municipal laws safely compartmented within their respective territories in order that they neither gradually merge nor eternally war with each other. The notion of national sovereignty has served all these purposes as a form of conceptual structuring agent.

The Act of State Doctrine is of a piece with the legal philosophy of its day. The Doctrine itself was formulated during the 1800s as a natural outgrowth of the international law theories of the "nationalist" writers. Intellectual fountainhead for the Doctrine is the territoriality-comity theory of international law, best stated by the Dutch writer Huber. His influential rules of "jurisdiction" are still the theoretical basis for private international law:

[2] Duke of Brunswick v. King of Hanover, 2 H.L.C. 1, 7 (1848).

1. The laws of each state have force within the limits of that government and bind all subject to it, but not beyond.

2. All persons within the limits of a government, whether they live there permanently or temporarily, are deemed to be subjects thereof.

3. Sovereigns will so act by way of comity that rights acquired within the limits of a government retain their force everywhere so far as they do not cause prejudice to the power or rights of such government or of its subjects.

Underlying these rules is the assumption of national autonomy over territory coupled with notions of high respect or deference among the nations for the official acts of the others. Rules 1 and 2 baldly state the territoriality principle, and Rule 3 tempers it with the comity doctrine. Joseph Story adopted these rules together with their underlying theories and in the early 1800s formulated his famous conflict of laws maxims from Huber's first two rules:

The first and most important general maxim or proposition is that which has been already adverted to, that every nation possesses an exclusive sovereignty and jurisdiction within its own territory.

Another maxim or proposition is, that no state or nation can by its laws directly affect or bind property out of its own territory, or bind persons not residents therein, whether they are natural born subjects or others.[8]

Professor Lorenzen noted in 1920 that these statements were not descriptively accurate at that time, nor even at the time Story published them.[4] They are no more accurate today. But their influence has been pervasive in American courts. The rules, of course, derive whatever intrinsic weight they may have from the heavy positive law content they carry.

The positivist jurisprudential conception of law as the "command of the sovereign" dovetailed neatly with the private international law notion that the essence of territorial

---

[8] Story, Conflict of Laws (8th ed. 1883) §§ 17, 18 and 20.

[4] Lorenzen, "Territoriality, Public Policy, and the Conflict of Laws," 33 Yale L. J. 736 (1924).

sovereignty consists in the physical ability of a given political ruler to compel obedience. The "analytical" school of jurisprudence founded by John Austin was concerned with this sort of law "properly so called." Thus to the positivist, international law is not law at all because there exists no agency superior to nation states possessing both authority and power to enforce obedience to commands. Arthur Nussbaum accurately describes the jurisprudential thought of the era in which the Act of State Doctrine was to emerge:

In the science of international law, the nineteenth century was the great era of positivism. . . . The science of international law was not definitely conceived as legal or juridical; it was severed from philosophy, theology, and considerations of policy, all of which had been ingredients of the law of nature. Generally, a clear line of demarcation was drawn between the actual law and the law of nations as it ought to be. Moreover, the art and techniques of diplomatic pursuits—that is, diplomacy—were distinguished from international law, which remained the competent discipline for the inquiry into legal relations of diplomatic agents. Differentiation was also pushed forward within the legal realm. The general inadequacy of private-law concepts in the problems of international law came to be recognized. . . . Private international law definitely attained the position of an independent discipline. . . .[5]

The philosophical superstructure erected upon this foundation led inexorably into the dualist concept of international law postulated by Triepel and still current today:

International law regulates between states, whereas municipal law is concerned with the relations between individuals (private law) or between individuals and the state itself (public municipal law). While municipal law is derived from the will of the particular state, international law finds its source in the common will of the states. International and municipal law are situated on different plains, as it were . . .[6]

Straightway from Huber to Story to Marshall the territoriality-comity theory can be traced, and in *Rose v.*

[5] Nussbaum, Concise History of the Law of Nations 233 (1954).
[6] *Id.* at 233.

Himely[7] and *Hudson v. Guestier*[8] the famous American Chief Justice made clear statements of the Anglo-American adaptation of the theory in the context of fact situations foreshadowing many to come later.

Natives on the island of Haiti in 1808 were in revolt against their French masters and had been mildly successful in their insurrection. The French governor by decree prohibited any trading with the rebels and authorized seizure of vessels within the territorial waters of Haiti caught violating the decree. An American-owned vessel, the *Rose Mary*, was seized on the high seas shortly after taking on a cargo from the rebels. The ship was brought before a French prize court sitting at nearby Spanish Cuba, and there ship and cargo were condemned and sold to another American shipmaster. The cargo later turned up in South Carolina, where the original owner libelled to recover it. Marshall held the seizure invalid in an exposition concerning international allocation of judicial competence: "It is conceded that the legislation of every country is territorial; that beyond its own territory, it can only affect its own subjects or citizens. It is not easy to conceive a power to execute a municipal law, or to enforce obedience to that law, without the circle in which that law operates."[9] Having cast the problem in pseudo-pragmatic terms concerning the vicissitudes of extraterritorial enforcement of judicial awards, he disposed of the lawsuit by noting that the seizure occurred outside Haitian waters, and the ship was never taken to Haiti at all:

If the court of St. Domingo had jurisdiction of the case, its sentence is conclusive. If it had no jurisdiction, the proceedings are *coram non judice*, and must be disregarded. Of its own jurisdiction, so far as depends on municipal rules, the court of a foreign nation must judge, and its decision must be respected. But if it exercise a jurisdiction which, according to the law of nations its sovereign could not confer, however available its

[7] Rose v. Himely, 8 U.S. (4 Cranch) 267 (1808). Compare Church v. Hubbard, 2 Cranch 187 (1804).

[8] Hudson v. Guestier, 8 U.S. (4 Cranch) 293 (1808).

[9] Rose v. Himely, *supra* note 7 at 278.

13

sentences may be within the dominions of the prince from whom the authority is derived, they are not regarded by foreign courts. This distinction is taken upon this principle, that the law of nations is the law of all tribunals in the society of nations, and is supposed to be equally understood by all.[10]

Accordingly, Marshall held the seizure and condemnation invalid, and thus the property title still resided with the original owner. The companion case (Hudson) involved similar facts, but the opposite result was reached because this particular vessel had been seized within French territorial jurisdiction.

Doctrinal statements foreshadowing the Act of State Doctrine appeared perhaps more clearly in a concise Marshall opinion arising from an international situation containing a more catastrophic political potential. Shortly after the success of the American Revolution there came a period in which counterrevolution was threatened. The British began making motions to reassert their control in North America. This would eventually culminate in the War of 1812. But during the years just prior to that small war the fledgling United States concluded a precarious peace with the mighty Napoleon and thereafter faced England with a little more confidence. Then occurred a potentially disastrous incident bearing directly on this peace pact. The schooner *Exchange*, privately owned by two American citizens, sailed from Baltimore to Spain in 1809 and was seized on the high seas in 1810 by French privateers who promptly converted her into an armed French ship-of-war. The French did not bother formally to condemn the ship as prize nor otherwise adjudicate a transfer of title. A year later the *Exchange* sailed into Philadelphia where the original owners libelled for restoration of their property. During the progress of the case through the courts the American Executive department filed a "suggestion" that, in view of the current American political alignment with the French, their "public vessel" should be allowed to come and go freely. The United

[10] *Id.* at 276.

14

States Supreme Court affirmed a district court dismissal of the libel, and the French kept the ship. But the interesting aspect of the case was the concept of national jurisdiction *circa* 1812 set forth in the following statement by Marshall:

The jurisdiction of the nation within its own territory is necessarily exclusive and absolute. It is susceptible of no limitation not imposed by itself. . . . The world being composed of distinct sovereignties, possessing equal rights and equal independence, whose mutual benefit is promoted by intercourse with each other, and by an interchange of those good offices which humanity dictates and its wants require, all sovereigns have consented to a relaxation in practice, in cases under peculiar circumstances, of that absolute and complete jurisdiction within their respective territories which sovereignty confers.[11]

He found that one such relaxation of sovereign jurisdiction existed with respect to armed warships of a foreign sovereign, and thus the *Exchange* sailed away still French.

These early American cases utilized the language of physical power to describe theories of international judicial jurisdiction, equating physical ability to enforce directly a judicial award with the judicial competence to decide a given controversy. This confusion of separate and distinct ideas remains an intrinsic part of American legal thought currently manifested by the almost insuperable conceptual problems concerning jurisdiction embodied in some of our current positivist law creations such as the Restatement of Conflict of Laws.

Another aspect of these early American cases is also important here. The heavy "political" context for these early decisions indicates the bearing which this factor exercised on the formulation of the Act of State Doctrine. The most important political event to the newly-emerged United States of America was peculiarly influential in this context:

The temporary dethronement of the Spanish Bourbon dynasty in the French-Spanish Campaign of 1808 kindled in the

[11] The Schooner Exchange v. McFaddon, 11 U.S. 116, 135-36 (1812).

Spanish-American colonies revolutionary movements which culminated in the formation of independent republics. . . . In connection with [the] planned intervention in Spain, the powers of the Holy Alliance had, at the Congress of Verona, envisaged intervention in the former Spanish colonies with a view to restore there the rule of the Spanish kings. To such schemes, Monroe, the President of the United States, in his message to Congress in 1822, declared firm opposition in what has become known as the Monroe Doctrine. Setting forth for the United States a policy of non-intervention in European conflicts, President Monroe announced—and this is the core of the Monroe Doctrine—that an attempt on the part of the allied powers (namely the members of the Holy Alliance) to extend their system to any portion of the Western Hemisphere would be considered as dangerous to the safety of the United States and that the latter would view any intervention by a European power for the purpose of oppressing the new American states or controlling in any other manner their destiny as "the manifestation of an unfriendly disposition toward the United States."[12]

The Monroe Doctrine was nothing more nor less than a mandate to the South American states to throw off their Spanish rule under the omnipresent protection of the United States. Uttered in the context of a series of revolutionary movements already in progress in South America, it was a policy statement which tended to further the process of those New World nations gaining their political independence, and, in fact, the statement manifested a hostility toward the Old World nations which was bound to encourage other dissident Latin Americans. The Monroe Doctrine thereby supplied the necessary national foreign policy foundation for the judicial Act of State Doctrine which was to be formulated before the nineteenth century ended.

The interrelationship of United States foreign policy and the Act of State Doctrine emerges even more clearly from the flow of judicial decisions arising from wars, revolutions, and nationalizations occurring in many different areas of the world during the twentieth century. The Doctrine was judicially created, framed, and applied most consistently

[12] Nussbaum, *supra* note 5 at 188.

16

and with greatest effect concerning events occurring in those areas which the Monroe Doctrine "protected" against the imperialist countries of Europe. But its usefulness was discovered not to be limited solely to our national relations with South American countries, and, subsequently, it came to be judicially applied in situations involving other foreign nations in order to implement our national policy of the moment concerning them.

2

MR. McKENNA: "Monroe was a statesman, an' he laid down this principle that if annywan, anny iv th' Powers—anny iv th' Eur-opean powers attempted to throw th' boots into anny counthry on this continent, we'd throw th' boots into thim."

MR. DOOLEY: "Well, I don't know Mon-roe, or whether he's a homypathy or on the square or a farryer; but I know a better doctorin. It's th' Hoolihan doctorin. . . . Niver stop to fight whin ye'er goin' to supper."

SOUTH AMERICAN SEIZURES

THE ACT OF STATE Doctrine was formulated against a background of United States foreign policy for South America and has been most vigorously applied in cases concerning events occurring south of the border. This aspect of the Doctrine was noted in 1929 by J. Scrutton, in the *Princess Paley Olga* case:

The United States situate in the neighborhood of South and Central American Republics, where the life of any Government is precarious and its death rarely by natural causes, frequently found in its territory property seized by a revolutionary force which ultimately succeeded in establishing itself in power and there sold the goods it had seized to persons who exported them to the United States, where they were claimed by their original owners.[1]

[1] Princess Paley Olga v. Weisz, 1 K.B. 718, 724 (1929).

With rare insight this judicial observation pinpoints the precise difference between the South American revolutions that spawned and gave basic content to the early Doctrine and its later applications to the pattern of transactions from the European area that, for the most part, embodied a pattern of attempted expropriation of assets located in or near this country. The South American nationalization cases involved seizures of movables located elsewhere which were subsequently brought within the jurisdiction of American courts where the lawsuit arose.

The Monroe Doctrine has been cited as the keystone of American foreign policy concerning the Latin American area. But it is by no criteria the last or even the best statement on this matter. One of the most cogent policy statements came in 1866 under the stress of genuinely threatening circumstances which lent an air of reality to the pronouncement. During the Civil War the major European powers took advantage of the fratricidal strife to attempt to reestablish their control in this hemisphere. On the grounds that the liberal revolutionary regime of Benito Juárez had failed to pay its debts, a multinational force sponsored by England, France, and Spain invaded Mexico in 1861. All of the invaders except France withdrew in 1862 following a guarded warning by the United States. But Napoleon III had in mind larger schemes than merely collecting his just debts. By 1864 his forces captured Mexico City and installed Archduke Maximilian of Austria as Emperor of Mexico. Rendered incapable of repelling Napoleon III by the Civil War, the United States pursued a realistic policy of placating him until Lee surrendered in April 1865. Less than a year later Secretary of State Seward informed the French minister that France should not delay withdrawal of her military forces from Mexico. His interpretation of our historic foreign policy deserves full quotation:

The practice of this government, from its beginning, is a guarantee to all nations of the respect of the American people for the free sovereignty of the people in every other state. We received the instruction from Washington. We applied it sternly in our early intercourse even with France. The same principle and practice have been uniformly inculcated by all our statesmen, interpreted by all our jurists, maintained by all our Congresses, and acquiesced in without practical dissent on all occasions by the American people. It is in reality the chief element of foreign intercourse in our history.[2]

Perversion of this fundamental policy eventually came in the McKinley-Roosevelt expansionist era of our history. This was followed closely by the "dollar diplomacy" of President Taft and his Secretary of State Philander C. Knox, which culminated in armed intervention in Nicaragua in 1912.[3] The utter bankruptcy of the dollar diplomacy approach to foreign relations with Latin America became distressingly patent, and the country returned to its fundamental foreign policy with President Woodrow Wilson.

Repudiation of dollar diplomacy policy with its concomitant of gunboat enforcement occurred within a few months after Wilson took office. It was first manifested by official disapproval in March 1913 of participating in a proposed private loan of $125 million to China by a group of American bankers, because of the possibility that it might result in "some unhappy contingency of forcible interference in the financial, and even the political, affairs of China which would be obnoxious to the principles upon which the government of our people rests." Similar explicit reversal of the policies of McKinley, Roosevelt, and Taft concerning Latin America followed a few months later. Speaking of the future and characterizing these nations as subject to exploitation through "concessions" to foreign capitalists, Wilson stated:

What these states are going to see, therefore, is an emancipating from the subordination, which has been inevitable, to foreign enterprise and an assertion of the splendid character which,

[2] H.R. Exec. Doc. No. 73, 39th Cong., 1st Sess., II, 348 (1866).
[3] Address of Hon. Philander C. Knox before New York State Bar Assoc. (1912), Foreign Rel. U.S., 1089-92 (1912).

21

. . . they have again and again been able to demonstrate. . . . They have had harder bargains driven with them in the matter of loans than any other people in the world. . . . Human rights, national integrity, and opportunity as against material interests . . . is the issue which we now have to face . . . the United States will never again seek one additional foot of territory by conquest.[4]

But Wilson found it exceedingly difficult to implement the policies of nonintervention. During his term of office the United States conducted an armed intervention in Haiti and the Dominican Republic, and our relations with Mexico were strained to the point of war.

The early South American revolutions in the 1800s were usually viewed favorably by the United States government, whereas the South American bankruptcies, wars, and revolutions of the early 1900s were politically disapproved by our government and often embarrassing for our stated foreign policy. The frequent changes in Latin American governments near the turn of the century called for a relatively inflexible judicial rule delimiting our national participation in these recurring matters.

The judicial Act of State Doctrine which resulted, however, rested upon three separate rationalizations. When the facts of the case involved foreign interference with the personal rights of an American citizen, domestic courts talked of "sovereign immunity"; if American-owned land was seized they spoke of "comity"; and if movables were involved they spoke of "vested rights" of property conferred by the foreign seizure.

THE SOVEREIGN IMMUNITY THEME

Foreign official acts which constituted interferences with the person have been treated by American courts as subject to an Act of State Doctrine in some manner analogous to the sovereign immunity privilege in international law. The

[4] S. Doc. No. 440, 63d Cong., 2d Sess. 5-8 (1914).

landmark opinion of Judge Wallace of the Second Circuit Court of Appeals in the *Underhill* case indicates this feature by invoking the idea that comity among nations demands that the conduct of a foreign state not be scrutinized by courts of another state because it might otherwise "vex the peace of nations":

Influenced by these reasons, and because the acts of the official representatives are the acts of the state itself, when exercised within the scope of their delegated powers, courts and publicists have recognized the immunity of public agents from suits brought in foreign tribunals for acts done within their own states in the exercise of sovereignty thereof.[5]

And in our earliest Act of State Doctrine case, the *Hatch* case, the sovereign immunity notion was expressed in the following passage explaining the basic reasons for the holding in that case:

The acts of the defendant for which he is sued were done by him in the exercise of that part of the sovereignty of St. Domingo which belongs to the executive department of that government. To make him amenable to a foreign jurisdiction for such acts would be a direct assault upon the sovereignty and independence of his country. . . . [But] the immunity of individuals from suits brought in foreign tribunals for acts done within their own states, in the exercise of the sovereignty thereof, is essential to preserve the peace and harmony of nations. . . .[6]

Not sovereign immunity itself but something very like it seems to be the substance of this form of Act of State Doctrine. The cases echo this theme.

[5] Underhill v. Hernandez, 65 Fed. 577, 570 (1895), *aff'd* 168 U.S. 250 (1897).
[6] Hatch v. Baez, 7 Hun 596 (N.Y. Sup. Ct. 1876).

Who	What	When	Where	Whither	Why
Hatch (Amer. nat'l) v. Baez (ex-Pres. of St. Domingo)[7]	Damages for assault in Santo Domingo	1876	N.Y. State	Baez wins	Sovereign Immunity or Act of State Doctrine
Underhill (Amer. nat'l) v. Hernandez (Venez. general)[8]	Damages for imprisonment in Venezuela	1895	Fed. Ct. in N.Y.	Hernandez wins	Sovereign Immunity or Act of State Doctrine
U.S. v. Watkins (Ger. nat'l) seized in Costa Rica[9]	Habeas corpus to escape deportation from United States	1947	Fed. Ct.	Watkins wins	Seizure lawful because of Act of State but deportation statute requirements not fulfilled
U.S. v. Watkins (Ger. nat'l) seized in Costa Rica[10]	Habeas corpus to escape deportation from United States	1947	Fed. Ct.	Watkins wins	Costa Rican citizenship valid under Act of State thus outside U.S. statute

[7] Ibid.
[8] Underhill v. Hernandez, supra note 5.
[9] U.S. v. Watkins, 159 F.2d 650 (1947).
[10] U.S. ex rel. Steinvorth v. Watkins, 159 F.2d 50 (1947).

THE INTERNATIONAL FULL
FAITH AND CREDIT THEME

The cases involving expropriation of land embody a form of Act of State Doctrine as a dispositive principle resembling the giving of full faith and credit to a foreign judgment. Three of these land cases were actually decided on matters of evidence, but our courts seem to adopt the foreign act of seizure as conclusive if it was attended by adjudication in a form satisfactory to the American forum. When it did not, however, as in the *Sabariego* case, the American court got quite adamant:

> If we had before us an actual and formal decree of a competent tribunal adjudging him guilty of the offence, and confiscating his property in punishment therefor, that of itself would not be sufficient to establish its own validity. We should still require record evidence of the existence of those facts which brought him and his property within the jurisdiction of the tribunal pronouncing such a decree. . . . This is a principle of natural justice, recognized as such by the common intelligence and conscience of all nations. A sentence of a court pronounced against a party, without hearing him or giving him an opportunity to be heard, is not a judicial determination of his rights, and is not entitled to respect in any other tribunal.[11]

The Act of State Doctrine was mentioned in the *Shapleigh* case, but the petitioners therein had conceded that if the Mexican expropriation decree were valid under Mexican law the Doctrine foreclosed any further inquiry—and so the point went without dispute. The American courts freely admitted they relied upon the foreign land law to determine land title questions, and the only inquiry was whether the particular seizure conformed to the municipal law of the situs at the time of taking. There was little else to do in most instances, for only in the *Shapleigh* case was alien-owned land involved, and the matter of possible invalidity under international law was expressly stipulated out of the case. Cases which exemplify the full faith and credit theme are:

[11] Sabariego v. Maverick, 124 U.S. 261, 292 (1888).

Who	What	When	Where	Whither	Why
Brownsville (Texas city) *v.* Cavazos (Mex. nat'l) [12]	Title to land now in U.S. seized by Mexico from defendant in 1826 when part of Mexico	1876	Fed. Ct. in Texas	Cavazos wins	Plaintiff failed to prove title because the Mexican confiscation was ineffective under Mexican law
Sabariego (Mex. nat'l) *v.* Maverick (Amer. nat'l) [13]	Land now in U.S. seized by Mexico, then sold to plaintiff	1888	Texas State Court	Maverick wins	Plaintiff failed to prove title because Mexican confiscation invalid
Amer. Banana Co. (Amer. corp.) *v.* United Fruit Co. (Amer. corp.) [14]	Treble damages under Sherman Act for land seized by Costa Rica for defendant	1908	Fed. Ct. in N.Y.	United Fruit wins	Sherman Act not applicable: Act of State by Costa Rica
Shapleigh (Amer. nat'l) *v.* Mier (Amer. nat'l) [15]	Title to land now in U.S. seized from the plaintiff by Mexico when part of Mexico	1937	Fed. Ct. in Texas	Mier wins	Plaintiff failed to prove invalid Mexican decree
Pasos (Amer. nat'l) *v.* Pan-American Airways (Amer. corp.) [16]	Damages for land seized by Nicaragua, then sold to defendant	1956	Fed. Ct. in N.Y.	Pan-American wins	No jurisdiction because "local" action and Act of State Doctrine

12 Brownsville *v.* Cavazos, 4 Fed. Cas. 460 (No. 2043) (1876), *aff'd* 100 U.S. 138 (1879).
13 Sabariego *v.* Maverick, *supra* note 11.
14 American Banana Co. *v.* United Fruit Co., 213 U.S. 248 (1908).
15 Shapleigh *v.* Mier, 83 F.2d 673 (1936), *aff'd* 299 U.S. 468 (1937).
16 Pasos *v.* Pan-American Airways, 195 F.Supp. 52 (U.S.D.C.S.D. N.Y., 1955), *aff'd* 229 F.2d 271 (CCA 1956).

THE RULE FOR DECISION THEME

The early cases from South America involving inter-ference with private movable property rights tended to defer to and thereby implement the application of foreign law despite the opposing claims of American nationals. Ostensibly this was done by means of a dogmatic version of the Act of State Doctrine grounded by the *Ricaud* opinion on the analogous sovereign immunity principle. Yet the "rule for decision" idea delineated in the *Ricaud* case makes this version of the Doctrine fall somewhere between the full faith and credit type of doctrine used in land cases and the sovereign immunity type of doctrine applied in the cases involving seizures of person. The property seizure version of Act of State does not afford a personal immunity from American court jurisdiction, but instead requires that jurisdiction be exercised to enforce the foreign law without inquiry by according the foreign governmental act conclusiveness as to the merits of the controversy. The foreign governmental seizure is considered to have transferred ownership as a matter of law, or perhaps as a matter of immutable fact. This version of the Doctrine seems to operate independently of the nationality of the particular parties.

Who	What	When	Where	Whither	Why
Oetjen (Mex. nat'l) v. Central Leather Co. (Amer. corp.) [17]	Hides seized in Mexico by revolutionaries, then sold by them to defendant	1917	N.J. State Court-U.S.	Central Leather Co. wins	Act of State Doctrine and no violation of Hague Rules of Land Warfare
Ricaud (Mex. nat'l) v. American Metals Co. (Amer. corp.) [18]	Lead bullion seized in Mexico by revolutionaries, then sold to plaintiff	1917	Fed. Ct. in Texas	Ricaud wins	Act of State Doctrine
Hewitt (Amer. nat'l) v. Speyer (Amer. corp.) [19]	Lien on funds located in U.S. paid by Ecuador to defendant	1918	Fed. Ct. in N.Y.	Speyer wins	Act of State Doctrine (suit in effect directed against Ecuador)
Terrazas (Mex. nat'l) v. Holmes Amer. nat'l) [20]	Cattle seized by Villa for Carranza gov't. in Mexico, then sold to defendant and brought to U.S.	1925	Texas State Court	Holmes wins	Diplomatic recognition of Carranza gov't plus Act of State Doctrine
Terrazas (Mex. nat'l) v. Donahue (Amer. nat'l) [21]	Cattle seized by Villa for Carranza gov't. in Mexico, then sold to defendant and brought to U.S.	1925	Texas State Court	Donahue wins	Act of State Doctrine
CIA Mineral Yendico Rodriguez Ramos S.A. (Mex. corp.) v. Bartlesville Lead & Zinc Co. and American Metals Co. (Amer. corp.) [22]	Damages for conversion by Villa in Mexico of 48 cars of ore now located in U.S.	1925	Texas State Court	CIA Mineral wins	Villa insurrection against Carranza failed—nonrecognition—Act of State Doctrine not available

Who	What	When	Where	Whither	Why
Eastern States Petroleum Co. (Amer. corp.) v. Asiatic Petroleum Co. (Amer. corp.) and El Aguila (Mex. corp.)[23]	Damages under Sherman Act and counterclaim against plaintiff by El Aguila for oil seizure in Mexico	1939	Fed. Ct. in N.Y.	Eastern States wins; El Agila counterclaim dismissed	Act of State Doctrine precludes inquiry into validity of Mexican law
Plesch (stateless) v. Banque Nationale de la Republique d'Haiti (Haiti state bank)[24]	Conversion of securities deposited in N.Y. with defendant, then transferred to Haiti	1948	N.Y. State Court	Plesch wins	Enforcement of Haitian confiscation decree against N.Y. public policy
Dix (Amer. nat'l, assignee of Ger. nat'l) v. Bank of Cal. Nat. Ass'n (Amer. corp.) and Honduras, Intervenor[25]	$6,727 in blocked account with defendant in U.S. from coffee export trade during World War II	1953	Fed. Ct. in Calif.	Honduras wins	Conflicts of law rule and Honduras law permitted extra-territorial operation of foreign exchange law
Frazier (Amer. nat'l) v. Foreign Bondholders Protective Council (Amer. ass'n)[26]	Damages for wrongful interference by defendant and Peru with bond contract between plaintiff and Peru	1953	N.Y. State Court	Foreign Bondholders Protective Council wins	FBP Council can rely on Act of State Doctrine as defense
Harris & Co. (Amer. nat'ls) v. Republic of Cuba[27]	Damages for breach of contract. Issue is validity of assets in U.S.	1961	Fla. State Court	Harris & Co. wins on Att. point	No sovereign immunity for Cuba's bank deposit in U.S. (Cuba's bank account not held ratione imperii)

Who	What	When	Where	Whither	Why
Pons (Cuban nat'l) v. Republic of Cuba[28]	Cuba sues for breach of contract; defendant counterclaimed for property seized in Cuba	1961	Fed. Ct.	Cuba wins	Act of State Doctrine bars counterclaim by Pons
Banco Nacional de Cuba (Cuban gov't bank) v. Sabbatino (Rec. for American-owned sugar co.)[29]	$175,000 proceeds from sugar seized in Cuba from subsidiary company and sold in N.Y.	1962	Fed. Ct. in N.Y.	Sabbatino wins	Cuban seizures in violation of international law, thus within exception to Act of State Doctrine

[17] Oetjen v. Central Leather Co., 246 U.S. 297 (1917).
[18] Ricaud v. American Metal Co., Ltd., 246 U.S. 304 (1917).
[19] Hewitt v. Speyer, 250 Fed. 367 (1918).
[20] Terrazas v. Holmes, 275 S.W. 392 (Tex. 1925).
[21] Terrazas v. Donahue, 275 S.W. 296 (Tex. 1925).
[22] CIA Mineral Yendico Rodriguez Ramos S.A. v. Bartlesville Lead & Zinc Co., 275 S.W. 388 (Tex. 1925).
[23] Eastern States Petroleum Co. v. Asiatic Petroleum Corp., 28 F. Supp. 279 (U.S.D.C.S.D.N.Y., 1939).
[24] Plesch v. Banque Nationale de la Republique d'Haiti, 77 N.Y.S.2d 43, 273 App. Div. 223 (1948).
[25] Dix v. Bank of California National Association, 113 F. Supp. 823 (CCA 10, 1952).
[26] Frazier v. Foreign Bondholders Protective Council, 125 N.Y.S.2d 900 (1953).
[27] Harris & Co. v. Republic of Cuba, 127 S.2d 687 (1961).
[28] Miguel Pons v. Republic of Cuba, 294 F.2d 925 (1962).
[29] Banco Nacional de Cuba v. Sabbatino, 193 F. Supp. 275 (U.S.D.C.S.D.N.Y., 1961), *aff'd* 307 F.2d 845 (CCA 2, 1962), *rev'd* 84 Sup. Ct. 923 (1964).

The overriding theme of all these South American seizure cases was not simply protection of American nationals, although that was accomplished whenever possible, but instead seems related to American foreign policy vis-à-vis the South American nations. Evident in the decision in *Sabariego* in 1888 was the underlying Monroe Doctrine, even though the Act of State Doctrine was yet to be judicially articulated. Miguel Losoya owned what is now downtown San Antonio which in 1811 was located in the Mexican state of Texas. He took part in a Mexican uprising against Spain thus provoking the Spanish government to seize his lands. In 1814 they were sold to a more loyal citizen named Garcia. Texas joined the United States in 1836, and thereafter some Americans (Maverick) occupied the land until 1888 when Garcia's descendants sued to recover it. The plaintiffs relied on a record title traced from the Spanish confiscation of the land but failed to convince the court it was a valid formal adjudication under the law of Mexico. The interesting aspect was the following passage from the opinion:

We are asked to assume that Miguel Losoya was guilty of the offense of treason against the King of Spain, and that he was so adjudged in regular judicial proceedings, on the basis of which conviction his property was officially seized and confiscated; and this we are asked to do as a judicial tribunal, sitting in a case wherein we are called to apply and administer the laws of Mexico, our government being the successor of that republic as the republic was the successor of the Spanish government, in order to justify the taking of Miguel Losoya's property and transferring it to another for the sole offense on his part of assisting to achieve the independence of his own country whose justice is now invoked against him.[30]

The American court refused to apply the foreign law, as one would suppose after reading that passage.

History establishes with persuasive clarity that our for-

[30] Sabariego v. Maverick, *supra* note 11 at 292.

eign relations policy concerning South America has strongly affected the judicial results of the cases arising in that area of the globe. These results were also influenced by certain other, more peculiarly judicial, considerations. But for the most part there is an arguably causal one-to-one relationship between our South American policy and the judicial outcomes. Mere contemporaneity does not establish causation: even a comprehensive sociological study designed to demonstrate the relationship of foreign policy to specific judicial outcome would not convince the unbelieving. A simple descriptive listing of these diplomatic and judicial events will have to suffice here.

The earliest series of South American seizure cases arose in the context of revolts by colonies against their European mother countries. Pre-Act of State Doctrine cases which qualify include *Hudson v. Guestier* and the *Rose Mary* cases which arose from the Haitian revolt led by Henri Christophe against France. The Act of State Doctrine cases arose from the context of similar revolts: Santo Domingo against France *(Hatch v. Baez)*, Mexico against Spain *(Cavazos* and *Sabariego)*, and most pointedly, Venezuela against Spain *(Underhill)*. The United States publicly approved of these revolts, and no better example of this can be cited than the fact that 1895, the same year that *Underhill* was decided, the United States aggressively opposed England and supported Venezuela in a boundary dispute. That same year Cuban rebel leaders who had survived the abortive ten-year Cuban revolt (which had begun in 1868) returned to Cuba and reinstituted their activities. This action provoked the Spanish to extreme retaliatory measures which were sensationally exploited by the American "yellow press" to whip up public outrage against Spanish misdeeds. Four years later the United States went to war with Spain over the whole matter of Spanish colonies in the Western hemisphere (and elsewhere).

Two years prior to *Underhill* the question of the Nicaraguan isthmian canal, which had been discussed as early as 1850, came to the forefront of public discussion in the United

States, heavily supported by the advocates of a strong American navy—Captain Mahan, Senator Henry Cabot Lodge, and Theodore Roosevelt. When Roosevelt became president upon the death of McKinley late in 1901, the canal project became preeminent in our South American policy. Congress chose Panama as the canal site in 1902 after a bitter debate, and Secretary of State John Hay executed a treaty with Colombia, which owned Panama, whereunder the price was $10 million outright plus $250,000 annually beginning nine years after ratification of the treaty. Colombia rejected the treaty in 1903, holding out for more money. Angered by Colombia's action, Roosevelt decided to take advantage of a fortuitous revolutionary plot to detach Panama from Colombia. When the revolution broke out in November 1903, the presence of American warships helped assure its success. Quickly recognizing the new Republic of Panama, the United States negotiated a treaty for construction of the canal. The *American Banana Co.* case arose shortly thereafter to be decided in 1908 on a theory which did not in any way cast suspicion on the United States' role in the Panama affair, the validity of our treaty, or the sovereignty of the Panamanian government. This category of South American cases also includes several late arising cases that stemmed from attempts by the United States to protect private American investments in South America made during the Roosevelt-Taft era and also bearing vaguely on the Panama Canal problem. A successful revolt in Nicaragua (1909) directed against the notorious dictator José Zelaya was supported by the United States. In order to assure the future financial solvency of both Nicaragua and Honduras following the success of the revolution, Wilson publicly encouraged private American bank loans to these new governments, to be secured by pledges of their customs duties and the whole financial matter to be administered by American officials. Another military intervention in Nicaragua by American Marines to "protect American financial interests" was conducted in 1912. Four years later *Hewitt v. Speyer* arose from a bondholder dispute concerning a private loan of this type to Ecuador, and as late as 1953 the case of *Frazier v. Foreign Bondholders Protective Council* involved a similar private loan to Peru.

Hard core Act of State Doctrine cases arose in the context of the long-continuing Mexican revolution. When the United States forced the French to withdraw military support from Maximilian, he was promptly executed by a Mexican firing squad in 1867. Ten years later Porfirio Díaz established a government and successfully held power until a revolution in 1911 brought to power the democrat Francisco Madero. Two Mexican land seizure cases arose during this period—*Sabariego* and *Brownsville v. Cavazos*. Then in 1913 the militarist dictator General Victoriano Huerta came to power. He executed Madero in February 1913. President Woodrow Wilson was even then in the process of publicly renouncing military intervention in South America as an acceptable instrument of American foreign policy, and he became personally incensed about the political murder of Madero. Huerta quickly gained effective control of Mexico and ignored Wilson's demanded settlement, whereupon Wilson declined to recognize the Huerta government and acrimonious relations ultimately led to American armed intervention in 1914 at Veracruz. Huerta was deposed by Venustiano Carranza who established a more democratic stable government. Pancho Villa and General Peneyra were Carranza generals during the revolution which the United States helped precipitate and covertly favored. The Carranza government was recognized by the United States in 1915, before the fighting had completely died out. The *Oetjen* and *Ricaud* cases arose from this phase of the Mexican revolution and were decided after the Carranza government had been formally recognized by this country. These seizures by a government which the United States Executive supported were supported by the Judicial branch. Pancho Villa attempted an unsuccessful revolution a few years later and seized properties which produced the two *Terrazas* cases and the *Bartlesville Lead and Zinc Co.* case. The Villa government was never formally recognized by this country because Villa never achieved de facto control of Mexico despite his exclusive holding of some of the northern-most Mexican states for several years. The final phase of the Mexican revolution came in the late 1930s when the oil industry was nationalized. Miraculously only the *Eastern States Petroleum Co.* case came before American courts by virtue of this seizure. There was strong pressure on the Executive to intervene in order to save American oil interests, but our overall national policy at this point was isolationism. The neutrality legislation of 1935 was the natural culmination of the isolationist policies of the 1930s and early in that decade manifested merely by a mandatory arms embargo statute. But it was part and parcel of the strong public feeling expressed by Senator Nye that America could have avoided involvement in World War I if we had exercised "a well-defined and strong neutrality policy at the beginning of the World War." Non-intervention to save American oil interests in Mexico ran closely parallel to this type of a policy of neutrality in the midst of the Depression.

A third wave of South American seizure cases came before American courts after World War II, most of them directly involving or impinging upon American wartime policies. The two *Watkins* cases involved the status of German nationals living in Costa Rica under United States deportation laws; the *Dix* case involved coffee export funds blocked in this country by virtue of United States wartime exchange controls; and the *Pasos* case in essence concerned title to Nicaraguan land originally seized by the government for use by American military forces. All these cases were obviously intimately related to American foreign policies during World War II.

A fourth wave of South American seizure cases arising from the Castro revolution in Cuba has now begun to show up in American courts. Whatever may have been the relationship between judicial outcomes in seizure cases and American foreign policies toward the Communist or the Nazi governments, history plainly reveals that the American judiciary has traditionally decided South American seizure cases consistently with our national policies concerning that area. The Judiciary has helped to implement those policies and, whenever possible, done so with reference not only to our fundamental foreign policy but also in the context of the proper role of the American judiciary in national life.

3

EUROPEAN SEIZURES

*J*UDICIAL TREATMENT accorded European seizures over the years reveals a predictable pattern of resistance to some foreign laws but not to others. This pattern is not at all in harmony with a rigorous "legal" application of accepted principles of law. Resistance to "Communist" law is clear and vigorous, but judicial antagonism is not so pronounced toward "Nazi" seizures. The international political relationship of a foreign nation with the United States at the time of the suit is one of the most important factors in foreign seizure lawsuits brought before American courts. For the most part, Communist seizure cases involved attempts to acquire control over assets located in this country. Thus these seizure cases could be judicially resisted by application of the extraterritoriality doctrine which generally prescribes that no nation can lawfully control assets located in another nation. Nazi seizures were directed toward assets in Europe that later turned up in this country, and the Act of State Doctrine was directly applied in these cases.

COMMUNIST EXTRATERRITORIAL CONFISCATIONS

American antipathy to Soviet law historically predates the current "cold war" period. It began with the October Revolution in 1917 and has continued throughout the past forty-nine years with only superficial deviations during the days of the "popular front" and the World War II military alliance against Hitler. The American courts were suspicious of the Soviets from the beginning and shared the general attitude of Western society: "In the twenties the Moscow communists had appeared to polite Anglo-Saxon society chiefly as a group of extremely bad-mannered people—anarchists and extremists, bristling with beards and bombs, misguided, motivated by all the wrong principles, unlikely to remain in power for any length of time, sure to be punished in the end for their insolent recalcitrance."[1] We felt that Soviet culture in general should be resisted, and a chronological survey of pertinent American judicial decisions indicates that our courts undertook to implement this animosity by resisting Soviet "law."

The judicial reaction to Soviet law initially took the form of a jurisdictional impediment, denying the Bolsheviks any "standing to sue" because they were not the "recognized" government of the Russian "state."

The refusal of the Executive department of the United States government formally to recognize the Russian "state" was the all-important factor in this context. The notorious "Black Tom" explosion case provided an early opportunity to initiate jurisdictional resistance.

[1] Kennan, Realities of American Foreign Policy (1954 Stafford Little Lecture Series at Princeton University) 24 (1954).

Early Soviet Seizures

The Imperial Russian Government had purchased a large quantity of munitions in this country, which were located on a Lehigh Valley Railroad train in Black Tom Terminal in Jersey City in 1916 when an explosion of incendiary origin destroyed them and devastated most of the surrounding territory. The Russian monarchy was overthrown shortly thereafter and in March 1917 the Kerensky (Provisional) government was recognized by the United States. Bakhmetieff was received here as the Russian ambassador. He sued the railroad company in 1918 seeking to recover the value of the Czar's munitions, but by this time (since October 1917) the Provisional government had been overthrown by Lenin's Bolsheviks. The railroad company sought to have the suit dismissed because Bakhmetieff had no authority to represent the new Bolshevik government and sought to prove the change in government because of the October Revolution. The State Department notified the court that Bakhmetieff was the "recognized ambassador of Russia" because the Communist government had not been recognized, and this persuaded the court to refuse proof of the downfall of the Provisional government. This ruling was affirmed on appeal, and certiorari was denied by the United States Supreme Court. Bakhmetieff finally recovered a money judgment in the suit, but the railroad company then complained that it might have to pay twice—once to Bakhmetieff and possibly again later to some Soviet ambassador after recognition. The court dragged in the Act of State Doctrine to deny this plea because "only the acts performed in its own territory . . . can be validated by the retroactive effect of recognition."[2]

Bakhmetieff remained the Russian ambassador until his retirement in 1922, whereupon Ughet, the Russian financial attaché, became official "custodian" of Russian property located in this country. The Bolsheviks had ruled as the de facto government of Russia for sixteen years; but the Pro-

[2] Lehigh Valley R. Co. v. Russia, 21 F.2d 396 (1927).

visional government having been previously "recognized" as representing the "state" of Russia, the international legal pantheon provided no place for another party also to represent Russia before the courts of this country. This state of affairs was carefully defined and polished in the *Wulfsohn*[3] and *Cibrario*[4] cases, in the latter of which the court noted: ". . . a foreign power brings an action in our courts not as a matter of right. Its power to do so is the creature of comity. Until such government is recognized by the United States, no such comity exists. The plaintiff concededly has not been so recognized. There is, therefore, no proper party before us."[5] This initial phase of American judicial resistance to Soviet law lasted from about 1917 until 1924 when the communists finally learned it was useless to continue sending their officials to litigate in American courts.

[3] Wulfsohn v. R.S.F.S.R., 193 N.Y. Supp. 472, *rev'd* 138 N.E. 24 (1923). (Soviet government can claim sovereign immunity from suits before American courts, thus cannot be made a defendant here.)

[4] Russian Socialist Federated Soviet Republic v. Cibrario, 191 N.Y. Supp. 543 (1923), 139 N.E. 259 (1923). Cibrario was employed in the United States as the purchasing agent for a Soviet agency, and while so employed he embezzled a large sum of money from his Soviet employer and deposited the money with the National City Bank in New York. The Soviet government sued him in New York state court in 1921 asking for an accounting and a receiver for his phony corporations. Cibrario defended that the Soviet government was unrecognized. The Soviets claimed to be the de facto government in Russia. The lower court held for Cibrario and the Soviet government appealed, prompting the landmark decision by the New York Court of Appeals based on a state public policy drawn by analogy from early Act of State cases. The upshot was that Cibrario got to keep the embezzled money.

The Cibrario case was instituted by one Ludwig C.A.R. Martens who appeared in the United States in 1917 claiming to be the official representative for the R.S.F.S.R. He was never officially received by the United States government and was finally deported in 1920. But before leaving he filed the Cibrario lawsuit and two others: The Rogdai, 278 F. 294 (1920) (libel action in California for possession of a ship owned by Russia in the possession of the Provisional government—dismissed because of nonrecognition); and The Penza, 277 F. 91 (1921) (libel for possession of two ships in New York being held by the Provisional government—dismissed because of nonrecognition and on the strength of the Act of State cases).

[5] *Id.* at 262.

The second line of resistance to Soviet law was to invoke local "public policy" against foreign confiscations[6] in order to avoid detrimental effects. The next series of Soviet nationalization cases passed through American state courts during 1924-1933 as lawsuits between private parties over property rights to valuables in which one litigant claimed rights under Soviet law. The jurisdictional gambit of denying the Soviets "standing to sue" was unavailable in these actions because no government representative was involved as a party. But, Soviet "law" was as objectionable as its representatives and a different legal device was required for American resistance. This set of legal factors prompted the American state courts to hold that Soviet law was offensive to the public policy of the several states.

The surface issues in most of these cases arose from the decreed "dissolution" of Russian corporations by the Soviets, and specifically involved the disposition of their corporate assets located in New York.[7] For the most part, litigation concerned with whether the corporation still "existed" or whether corporate debts were effectively cancelled by the confiscations was determined by judicial declarations that the Soviet decrees had no extraterritorial effect, and thus whoever asserted their applicability to local corporate assets

[6] The Kerensky government in Russia was overthrown by the Bolsheviks early in November 1917 and the R.S.F.S.R. thereafter decreed confiscation of all land (Nov. 7, 1917) and "underground depths" (Nov. 8, 1917) established "workmen's control over production, purchase, sale of products and raw materials, their storage, and also over the financial side of the enterprise" (Nov. 27, 1917) and prohibited all settlements of payments abroad under any private contracts (Sept. 14, 1918); then annulled "all shares, bonds, and securities which might be in the possession of Russian or foreign private holders" (June 28, 1918) and nationalized soap factories (June 28, 1918) and "all industrial enterprises" having over 5 workmen and a certain capitalization (Nov. 29, 1920). Banks and insurance companies were nationalized in 1917, 1918, and 1919. Sacks, "The Diplomatic Claims of the Soviets," 16 N.Y.U.L. Rev. 253 (1939).

[7] Nebolsine, "Recovery of the Foreign Assets of Nationalized Russian Corporations," 39 Yale L. J. 1130 (1930); Bergstrom, "Effect of Confiscation Decrees on American Assets of Russian Companies after Recognition," 88 Univ. Pa. L. Rev. 116 (1939).

41

lost his case. So long as a goodly number of exiled Russian directors still lived, American courts could plausibly maintain that "disembodied corporations," American subsidiaries of dead Russian parents, still lived for legal purposes. But as the years passed on, so did the directors until by 1931 in the *Severnoe* case only two directors were still alive, and the fiction wore too thin. Another legal contention was raised by various American deposit agents who expressed fears that they might be subject to double liability if they remitted "confiscated" funds or securities to their Russian depositors and at some future time found themselves liable for these funds to a "recognized" Soviet government. New York courts expressly cited this theory in several cases. Yet a New York statute which permitted an indefinite stay in such suits in order to avoid this possibility was judicially invalidated in 1925.

The Act of State Doctrine was applied expressly in only two of these cases and may have been the unexpressed rationale for a third. Both the *Salimoff* and *Dougherty* opinions seemed to rely on the Doctrine, expressly or impliedly, although the stated dispositive theory for each was simply the situs rule of private international law plus a finding that no local public policy was offended since only Russian nationals were deprived by the seizures. On the other hand, the *Banque de France* case may be one of the few American Act of State decisions involving a clear international delinquency, although nothing was made of it at the time. The following table lists the significant cases involving disposition of corporate assets in New York of Russian companies.

Who	What	When	Where	Whither	Why
Sokoloff (Russian nat'l) v. Nat. City Bank (Amer. corp.)[8]	$28,365 deposited in Russian branch of defendant bank	1924	N.Y. State Court	Sokoloff wins	Extraterritoriality (Amer. bank's liability not affected by USSR act)
Russian Reinsurance Co. (Russ. corp.) v. Stoddard (N.Y. Ins. Comm.)[9]	Securities deposited in Bankers Trust Co. (N.Y.)	1925	N.Y. State Court	Stoddard (Bankers Trust) wins	Possible double liability of Bankers Trust
Fred S. James & Co. (Amer. corp.) assignee of Eagle Star Ins. Co. (Brit. corp.) v. Second Russian Ins. Corp.[10]	Marine ins. claims owned by Sec. Russ. claimed to be cancelled by USSR decrees	1925	N.Y. State Court	James & Co. wins	Extraterritoriality (Soviet decrees cancelling defendant's debts not operative outside Russia)
Joint-Stock Co. (Russ. corp.) v. Nat. City Bank (Amer. corp.)[11]	$5,000 deposited in U.S.	1925	N.Y. State Court	Joint-Stock wins	Extraterritoriality (Soviet decrees confiscating plaintiff's deposit not operative outside Russia)
Sliosberg (Russ. nat'l) v. N.Y. Life Ins. Co. (Amer. corp.)[12]	Suit for surrender value of 16,140 rubles where defendant claims indefinite stay under N.Y. statute	1925	N.Y. State Court	Sliosberg wins	N.Y. statute unconstitutional because it impairs contracts
James & Co. (Amer. corp.) assignee of Eagle Star Co. (Brit. corp.) v. Russia Ins. Co. (Russ. corp.)[13]	Claims under reinsurance contract where plaintiff claims transfer of assets from Russian parent corp. to defendant was fraudulent	1928	N.Y. State Court	Russia Ins. Co. wins	Not fraudulent transfer because conservatory measure to escape confiscation

Who	What	When	Where	Whither	Why
Banque de France (Fr. state bank) v. Equitable Trust Co. Amer. corp.)[14]	$2.6 million in French gold seized by Soviets in Russia and transferred to German bank which deposited with defendant in U.S.	1929	Fed. Ct. in N.Y.	Equitable Trust wins	Act of State Doctrine and possible double liability of American depository
Severnoe Securities Corp. (Amer. corp.) assignee of Russ. corp. v. London & L. Ins. Co. (Brit. corp.)[15]	Claim on policy where defendant attacks plaintiff's standing to sue because assignor dissolved by Soviet decrees	1931	N.Y. State Court	London & L. Ins. Co. wins	Russ. corp. has only two surviving directors—suit should be in England where they live
Re People by Beha (Russ. Reins. Co.) & First Russ. Ins. Co. v. Beha, N.Y. State Ins. Comm'r[16]	$2 million assets available for liquidation distribution	1931	N.Y. State Court	Directors of Russ. Reins. Co. & First Russ. Ins. win	N.Y. state has no further interest because all local claims paid
Salimoff & Co. (Russ. nat'ls) v. Standard Oil Co. (Amer. corp.)[17]	Accounting for oil seized in Russia and sold to Standard Oil which resold abroad	1933	N.Y. State Court	Standard Oil wins, relying on Soviet law	1) Situs rule of conflicts of law 2) Seizure not against N.Y. public policy 3) Act of State Doctrine (make-weight)

Who	What	When	Where	Whither	Why
Dougherty (26 Russ. nat'ls representing 6,000 policy holders) v. Equitable Life Assur. Soc. (Amer. corp.)[18]	Return of premiums on cancelled policies and seized surrender values	1933	N.Y. State Court	Equitable Life wins, relying on Soviet law	1) Situs rule of conflicts of law (law of the contract was Russia) 2) Act of State Doctrine (unexpressed make-weight) 3) Seizure not against N.Y. public policy

8 Sokoloff v. National City Bank, 145 N.E. 917 (1924).
9 Russian Reinsurance Co. v. Stoddard, 240 N.Y. 149 (1925).
10 Fred S. James & Co. v. Second Russian Ins. Corp., 146 N.E. 369 (1925).
11 Joint-Stock Co. v. National City Bank, 240 N.Y. 368, 148 N.E. 552, *affirming* 210 App. Div. 665, 206 N.Y. Supp. 476 (1925).
12 Sliosberg v. New York L. Ins. Co., 244 N.Y. 482, 155 N.E. 740, *cert. denied* 275 U.S. 526 (1927).
13 James & Co. v. Russia Ins. Co., 247 N.Y. 262 (1928).
14 Banque de France v. Equitable Trust Co., 33 F.2d 202 (1929).
15 Severnoe Securities Corp. v. London & L. Ins. Co., 255 N.Y. 120, 174 N.E. 299 (1931).
16 Re People by Beha, 255 N.Y. 433, 175 N.E. 120 (1937) *reversing* 243 N.Y. Supp. 35, *rehearing* 185 N.E. 766, 261 N.Y. 624 and 262 N.Y. 455, 199 N.E. 17 (1933).
17 Salimoff v. Standard Oil Co., 186 N.E. 679 (1933).
18 Dougherty v. Equitable Life Assur. Soc., 193 N.E. 897 (1923).

45

Judicial antagonism to the Soviet confiscatory laws was the omnipresent theme of these disposition cases. Sometimes the attitude was so compelling the state court acknowledged it expressly. In the *Sliosberg* case antipathy was strong enough to emasculate a New York statute which ran counter to it. The statute permitted an indefinite stay of judicial proceedings in particular cases pending diplomatic recognition of the Soviets by the United States government. But the court invalidated the statute because:

[W]e do not think that the public weal requires that honest creditors should be made to abide the time when a law, inherently unjust and confiscatory, enacted by a governmental power then regarded as barbarous, might become an effective weapon of defense through the recognition of that power as a worthy member of the society of civilized nations.[19]

But in most cases opposition to Soviet law took the form of protecting American nationals against the direct effects of the foreign law. The courts were often candid about their protectionist rulings. The most outright expression of protectionism is the *Banque de France* case in which the American defendant was relying on the Soviet title to $2.6 million in French gold seized in Russia in 1918 and subsequently deposited in a German bank which shipped the gold to this country. The French sued in this country, and the Americans raised the Act of State Doctrine as a defense.

This would seem to present a clear Act of State case, but because the Soviets were an unrecognized government the court grounded its ruling on a more "fundamental" reason:

To deprive these defendants who are American nationals of asserting title to gold which was shipped to them to be in the State Bank, and to preclude the defendants from showing in what manner such title was acquired, I believe would be doing violence to fundamental justice and would be contrary to the principles which the courts of this country apply. . . . Justice requires that effect should be given by our courts, even though we do not recognize the Russian government, to those acts in

[19] Sliosberg v. New York L. Ins. Co., *supra* note 12 at 755.

Russia upon which the rights of our citizens depend, provided [there is no encroachment on the political branch].[20]

This protective attitude was apparent also in the *Second Russian Ins. Co.* case where the American plaintiff was the assignee of a British firm who brought a claim against a Russian corporation and the latter invoked the Soviet laws cancelling its foreign debts: "Neither comity nor public policy requires us to enforce a mandate of confiscation at the behest of such a government [unrecognized] to the prejudice either of our own citizens or of those of any friendly power seeking justice in our courts."[21] On the other hand, the theme was often present although unexpressed in the opinion. The two most notorious examples are *Salimoff* (involving oil seized by the Soviets and sold to Standard Oil) and *Dougherty* (involving "confiscated" insurance values) where "foreign law" was deliberately applied to allow the American defendants to prevail over the foreigners:

[Salimoff]—A recovery in conversion is dependent upon the laws of Russia. . . . When no right of action is created at the place of wrong, no recovery in tort can be had in any other State on account of the wrong.[22]

[Dougherty]—[I]t cannot be against the public policy of this State to hold nationals to the contracts which they have made in their own country to be performed there according to the laws of that country.[23]

There were a few clear exceptions to the policy of protecting American nationals. In the *Sokoloff* and *Sliosberg* cases the foreign national won over his American opponent, but these instances merely reinforce the primary theme of judicial antagonism to Soviet law. In both instances the American litigant who lost the case was relying heavily on the validity

[20] Banque de France v. Equitable Trust Co., *supra* note 14 at 206-208.
[21] Fred S. James & Co. v. Second Russian Ins. Co., *supra* note 10 at 321.
[22] Salimoff v. Standard Oil Co., *supra* note 17 at 682.
[23] Dougherty v. Equitable Life Assur. Soc., *supra* note 18 at 903.

of the Soviet confiscatory decrees as the legal basis for his claim and these courts were unwilling to permit Soviet "law" to prevail regardless who invoked it.

In doctrine, there was no single, clear rule invoked to effect these policies. The court in the *Joint-Stock Co.* case characterized the Soviet decrees as punitive and thus strictly territorial in application. Nonrecognition played a part in most of the decisions but more as a make-weight than anything else. This seemed to be clearly perceived by Mr. Justice Cardozo in the *Sokoloff* case when he discussed the possibility of giving effect to the laws of a de facto government if to do so would suit our public policy and vice versa. And the most succinct statement of the ever-popular extraterritoriality doctrine appears in the *Second Russian Ins. Corp.* case where the technical issue—as in most of the cases of this group—was whether the Soviet decrees had dissolved the Russian corporation for all judicial purposes:

The decree of the Russian Soviet government nationalizing its insurance companies has no effect in the United States unless, it may be, to such extent as justice and public policy require that effect be given. . . . The defendant asks us to declare its death as a means to the nullification of its debts and the confiscation of its assets by the government of its domicil.[24]

The larger issue at stake in these cases was whether Soviet law or New York state law would be given effect in judicially administering the assets located in the United States consisting of the dollar residues of dissolved Russian corporations. Normally, this question could be resolved by deciding that the Soviet decrees should be given no extraterritorial effect. Where the extraterritoriality rule was inapplicable, however, nonrecognition of the Soviets coupled with New York state public policy against "confiscations" were judicially combined to protect the economic interests of American nationals. From these cases came the generaliza-

[24] Fred S. James & Co. v. Second Russian Ins. Corp., *supra* note 10 at 370.

tion that foreign seizures of private property were against our public policy and that the foreign law would thus be given no extraterritorial effect in this country.

Soviet Seizures since Diplomatic Recognition

The American-Soviet rapprochement in 1933 put an end to this stage of the relationship, and thereafter an altered political and judicial course was set. This diplomatic turn was signalled when Ughet was dismissed by the United States government in 1933 and the Soviet government was officially recognized by the American government. The first Soviet ambassador, Maxim Litvinov, came to the United States soon thereafter and, through an exchange of letters with President Roosevelt, assigned to the American government the Soviet claims to assets located here. The "popular front" was soon in full swing. Formal recognition of the Soviet government undercut the primary theory then being used by American courts to oppose Soviet law, and the Litvinov assignment itself thrust the federal government into the lawsuits which were still dragging through the state courts.

This extreme diplomatic turn was too great for the American state courts to follow. They either failed to realize that the old era had passed or chose to ignore the shift in Executive policy. The New York courts were not favorably impressed by the Litvinov assignment and continued to decide the various lawsuits so as to minimize the local effect of the Soviet laws and protect American nationals whenever possible—all in the name of New York "public policy." It was difficult for them to hold in favor of American nationals in most of these cases because the funds involved consisted of the remainder of deposits in this country after all local creditors of the Russian companies had been paid in full and the suits were between the American deposit agent and foreign creditors (whose claims arose from the foreign business of the defunct Russian companies). After the Litvinov assignment this was complicated by the fact that the United States government was also a party to the suits. The larger issue in these cases was whether the United States government or the state of New York would administer the final distribution of these sums. The federal plans generally advocated using the money as a form of "lump sum settlement" for foreign creditors' claims and the New York courts contemplated remitting the money to the émigré directors. A decided shift in the pattern of judicial results is clearly observable following these events.

Who	What	When	Where	Whither	Why
Moscow Fire Ins. Co. (Russ. corp. representing foreign creditors) v. Bank of N.Y. Trust Co. (Amer. corp.) and U.S., Intervenor[25]	$1,080,399 in liquidation assets in N.Y.	1933	N.Y. State Court	Moscow Fire Ins. Co. wins	1) USSR decrees did purport to apply to N.Y. assets 2) Extraterritoriality 3) Act of State distinguished 4) Recognition immaterial
Vladikavkazsky Ry. (Russ. corp.) v. N.Y. Trust Co. (Amer. corp.)[26]	$46,584 deposited in N.Y. by plaintiff to back bonds sold to U.S. citizens	1934	N.Y. State Court	Vladikavkazsky Ry. wins	Extraterritoriality (corp. still in existence here)
U.S. v. Guaranty Trust Co. (Amer. corp.)[27]	$5 million deposited by Russ. Prov. Gov't.	1938	Fed. Ct. in N.Y.	Guaranty Trust Co. wins	Statute of limits had run on claim assigned by Soviets to U.S.
U.S. v. Belmont (N.Y. bank)[28]	$1 million deposited in N.Y. with defendant as stockholder for Russ. corp.	1938	Fed. Ct. in N.Y.	U.S. wins	1) Litvinov assignment 2) Recognition and Fed. supremacy bar N.Y. 3) Act of State bars Russ. corp.
U.S. v. Pres. and Directors of the Manhattan Co. (Amer. corp.)[29]	$332,994 deposited with defendant by directors of North Ins. Co. of Moscow (liquidated)	1938	N.Y. State Court	U.S. wins	1) Litvinov assignment 2) Private claimant not authorized to hold money because only 2 of 5 Russ. directors acted

Who	What	When	Where	Whither	Why
Petrogradsky M. K. Bank (Russ. corp.) v. Nat. City Bank (Amer. corp.)[30]	$66,749 deposited in N.Y. by plaintiff	1940	N.Y. State Court	Petrogradsky Bank wins	Extraterritoriality (corp. still exists here)
U.S. (claiming for U.S. claimants against USSR on other matters) v. Pink (N.Y. Supt. of Ins. claiming for foreign claimants of First Ins. Co.)[31]	$1 million in liquidation assets deposited in Bank of N.Y. Trust under N.Y. court order (for Russ. creditors of First Ins. Co.)	1942	Fed. Ct. in N.Y.	U.S. wins	1) Litvinov assignment 2) Recognition 3) Extraterritorial effect honored by analogy to Act of State 4) Federal supremacy
U.S. v. N.Y. Trust (Amer. corp.)[32]	$78,759 deposited by Russ. railroad with defendant in N.Y.	1946	Fed. Ct. in N.Y.	U.S. wins	Litvinov assignment and no setoff by defendant because of sovereign immunity

[25] Moscow Fire Ins. Co. v. Bank of N.Y. Trust Co., 280 N.Y. 286, 20 N.E.2d 758 (1939), *aff'd* 309 U.S. 624 (1940).

[26] Vladikavkazsky R. v. N. York Trust Co., 263 N.Y. 369, 189 N.E. 456 (1934).

[27] Guaranty Trust Co. v. U.S., 304 U.S. 126 (1938).

[28] U.S. v. Belmont, 301 U.S. 324 (1938).

[29] U.S. v. President and Directors of the Manhattan Co., 12 N.E.2d 518 (1938).

[30] Petrogradsky M.K. Bank v. National City Bank, 253 N.Y. 23, 170 N.E. 479 (1940).

[31] U.S. v. Pink, 315 U.S. 203 (1942).

[32] U.S. v. New York Trust, 75 F. Supp. 583 (U.S.D.C.S.D.N.Y., 1946).

The American defendant in the *Petrogradsky* case raised the claim that the Russian corporation had been dissolved in Russia and thus was not a juridical person, but the court noted "the decrees of the Soviet Republic nationalizing Russian banks are not law in the United States, nor recognized as law." This express reliance on Soviet law by a claimant was carefully avoided by the next American defendant in the *Vladikavkazsky* case, however, and only good New York law was cited in support of substantially the same legal position. The court saw through the gambit and held that even formal recognition of the Soviets by the United States government did not override the public policy of New York against the Soviet confiscations. Even after the federal government got into the lawsuits the state courts held to their course. In the *Moscow Fire Ins. Co.* case the court noted that "foreign law is of effect here only in so far as the federal supremacy dictated national policy in the field of foreign affairs," yet in those areas "outside of that field the State determines its own public policy and embodies it in its own law." Quotation from the *Manhattan Co.* case embodies the substance of the attitude:

It is clear that we would not in this forum recognize the confiscation decree of 1918 to the end that the Soviet government or its assignee might assert title to the assets of the foreign corporation within our jurisdiction to the prejudice of our own nationals who are creditors.[33]

The federal government asserted the Act of State Doctrine in support of its claims, contending that the diplomatic recognition retroactively validated the Russian decrees, but the state courts distinguished the factual situation in which seizure occurs abroad from cases in which the property had always been located inside New York State. Both the federal government and the state court held to these positions in the *Pink* case, and it was sent to the U.S. Supreme Court to

[33] U.S. v. President and Directors of the Manhattan Co., *supra* note 29 at 523.

decide the matter. Mr. Justice Douglas seemed to concede *sub silentio* the force of the state court's legalistic demarcation in his opinion in the *Pink* case, but he adroitly sidestepped the matter and attacked frontally the distinction attempted by the New York court in the *Moscow Fire Ins. Co.* case which had attempted to parcel out the "policy" areas between the states and the federal government. Justice Douglas wrote:

Enforcement of New York's policy as formulated by the Moscow case would collide with and subtract from the federal policy, whether it was premised on the absence of extraterritorial effect of the Russian decrees, the conception of the New York branch as a distinct juristic personality, or disapproval by New York of the Russian program of nationalization. . . . Such action by New York, no matter what gloss be given it, amounts to official disapproval or nonrecognition of the Soviet government. . . . It is in the face of the underlying policy adopted by the United States when it recognized the Soviet government . . . it helps keep alive one source of friction which the policy of recognition intended to remove. . . . Certainly, the conditions for "enduring friendship" between the nations, which the policy of recognition in this instance was designed to effectuate, are not likely to flourish where, contrary to national policy, a lingering atmosphere of hostility is created by state action.[34]

He then brought forth the Act of State Doctrine to support this position by analogy. Adverting to principles allegedly common to situations involving foreign seizures of assets located outside this country and also to foreign governmental seizures of assets located inside this country followed by diplomatic agreement concerning them, Mr. Justice Douglas ruled that in the conduct of national foreign affairs Executive Agreements override a state's public policy.

The *Pink* case resolved the immediate controversy over whose "policy" controlled as between New York and the federal government. But because of the underlying Executive Agreement the case actually represents an exceptional situation. The main flow of cases applying the Act of State Doc-

[34] U.S. v. Pink, *supra* note 31 at 231.

trine does not involve treaties or other types of international agreements.

The events of the World War II era shifted the focus from the law of Russia proper to the law of the other countries of Eastern Europe, where the initial pattern of seizures took a more subtle form. Soviet occupation of the Baltic countries in the summer of 1940 was followed by their political "absorption" and by nationalization of Lithuanian, Estonian, and Latvian companies. Seizure of these companies was effected by coercing the individual owners to sign over their businesses to Soviet designees. Thereafter the designee attempted to obtain possession of the overseas assets, primarily ships, by asserting his "ownership" abroad. The United States Executive department refused to "recognize" the sovietization of these countries, and this form of nonrecognition became the doctrinal core of the response of American courts. The precise technical issue was raised in the first three of these cases by the defendant's allegation that the Soviet designee's "title" was obtained by coercion and was thus invalid. Inquiry into this issue led ultimately to the "unrecognized" Soviet government takeover and thus blocked Soviet attempts to obtain the ships. The cases in which this judicial position was worked out are:

Who	What	When	Where	Whither	Why
Silberberg (Soviet designee) v. Kaiv (Estonian consul in exile)[35]	Libel for the *Kotkas* and the *Regent* (Estonian ships)	1940	Fed. Ct. in N.Y.	Estonian consul in exile wins	1) Soviet designee failed to prove paper "title" 2) Nonrecognition 3) American "freezing" orders
Baltic Lloyd, Lietukis, Latvian State Cargo Line (Soviet corps.) v. Litamcor (Amer. corp.)[36]	Libel for the *Denny* (Lithuanian ship) plus claim for damages	1941	Fed. Ct. in N.Y.	In rem action dismissed but damage claim permitted	1) Ownership proved 2) Act of State Doctrine 3) Only Lithuanians involved
Tiedemann (Soviet designee) & Estonian State Steamship Line (Soviet corp.) v. Kaiv (Estonian consul in exile)[37]	Libel for the *Signe* (Estonian ship)	1943	Fed. Ct. in New Orleans	Estonian consul in exile wins	1) Soviet designee failed to show paper "title" 2) Nonrecognition 3) Estonia now under Nazi occupation
Amtorg Trading Corp. (Soviet corp.) v. Kaiv (Estonian consul in exile)[38]	Reimbursement from compensation fund of $15,187 in advances for provisions made under Soviet orders after purported nationalization of ship in Virgin Islands	1944	Fed. Ct. in Calif.	Amtorg gets only a portion of the sum claimed	1) Nonrecognition, thus 2) Soviet decrees inoperative, thus 3) Advances not authorized by "owner"

Who	What	When	Where	Whither	Why
Latvian State Cargo Steamship Lines (Latvian state corp. represented by Soviet designee) v. McGrath (U.S. Alien Property Custodian)[39]	Insurance proceeds from sinking of ship belonging to confiscated Latvian private corp.	1945	Fed. Ct. in N.Y.	McGrath wins	1) Nonrecognition 2) *Pink* and *Belmont* cases relied upon

[35] The Kotkas & The Regents, 35 F. Supp. 983-85 (1940).

[36] The Denny, 127 F.2d 404 (1942).

[37] The Florida, 133 F.2d 719 (1943).

[38] The Maret, 145 F.2d 431 (1944).

[39] Latvian State Cargo & Passenger Steamship Lines v. McGrath, 188 F.2d 1000 (1951).

The cases from the later Eastern European nationalizations arising after World War II during the "cold war" period of the early 1950s were factually more complex, but they manifested the same resistance to Communist law. The defendants in these cases relied upon foreign law for their rights and cited the Act of State Doctrine to prevent judicial inquiry. None of these decisions permitted the foreign law to prevail despite the Act of State Doctrine, except in the one instance in which the economic interests of an American national would have been threatened by this approach; so it was not used, and thus in *Tsuk v. New York Trust Co.* the decision was doctrinally muddled. The court nevertheless effectively protected the American corporate stockholder against the claims of the Hungarians who were the original owners of the money deposited in this country. The following are cases in which these domestic owners were protected:

Who	What	When	Where	Whither	Why
Sulyok (Hung. nat'l) v. Penintezetz Kospowt Budapest (Hung. state bank)[40]	Damages for breach of employment contract with defendant in Hungary (defendant claimed Act of State)	1952	N.Y. State Court	Sulyok wins	Sulyok not Hungarian at time of decree; Act of State Doctrine not applicable; decree against N.Y. public policy
Tsuk (Hung. nat'ls) v. Kuerschner & Rauchwarenfabrik (Hung. corp.) and N.Y. Trust Co. (Amer. corp.)[41]	$9,800 deposited with defendant in U.S. as frozen funds (defendant moved to dismiss Tsuk, ex-owners)	1954	Fed. Ct. in N.Y.	N.Y. Trust Co. wins	Defendant should not risk double liability
Capitol Records (Amer. corp.) assignee of Telefunken (Ger. corp.) v. Mercury Record Corp. (Amer. corp.) assignee of Gramophone (Czech corp.)[42]	Declaratory judgment that performance rights in U.S. belonged to Telefunken rather than to Gramophone	1955	Fed. Ct. in N.Y.	Capitol Records wins	Extraterritoriality (Czech confiscation of record matrices did not give performance rights in U.S.)
Zwack (Hung. nat'l) v. Kraus Bros. & Co. (Amer. corp.)[43]	$17,000 in defendant's hands in U.S. as agent of plaintiff; injunction on trademark use (defendant claimed Act of State)	1956	Fed. Ct. in N.Y.	Zwack wins	1) Plaintiff has standing despite Act of State 2) Foreign confiscations against public policy 3) No extraterritorial effect permitted

Who	What	When	Where	Whither	Why
Stevens (Rec. for Czech bank) v. Zivnostanka Banka (Czech bank) and State Bank of Czechoslovakia[44]	Money on deposit to defendant's account in N.Y. banks	1960	N.Y. State Court	Stevens wins	Czech decrees against N.Y. public policy, thus no extra-territorial effect permitted

[40] Sulyok v. Penintezetz Kospowt Budapest, 111 N.Y. Supp.2d 75, 279 App. Div. 528 (1952).

[41] Kuerschner & Rauchwarenfabrik v. N.Y. Trust Co., 126 F. Supp. 684 (U.S.D.C.S.D.N.Y., 1954).

[42] Capitol Records v. Mercury Record Corp., 113 F. Supp. 330 (1952), *aff'd* 221 F.2d 657 (CCA 2, 1955).

[43] Zwack v. Kraus Bros. & Co., 133 F. Supp. 929, *aff'd* 237 F.2d 255 (1956).

[44] Stevens v. Zivnostanka Banka, 199 N.Y.S.2d 797 (1950).

The post-World War II phase of this type of litigation in Eastern Europe has been perceptively surveyed by Grzybowski who incorporates not only the cases here reported but additional ones on related points, all correlated with the principles established from the previous phases of the American-Soviet judicial interactions stemming from the Russian confiscations of 1917. He summarizes thus:

The territorial expansion of the Soviet Union and the spread of Soviet law and government in Eastern Europe, have multiplied the number of cases which call for decision on the extent to which Soviet and satellite law may be effective in other countries. Broadly speaking, problems of conflict of law arising in this connection have originated in the treatment of property rights under communist legislation. They are quite similar to those which arose from the Russian legislation that came before the courts of other countries after World War I.[45]

He relates the fascinating phenomenon of the gradual disintegration of unitary German "law" under the impact of the political (and philosophical) separation of East and West Germany and relates this to the international process of resistance to Soviet law which the American courts have manifested since 1917. The principal legal device for nullifying the effect of Soviet law in West Germany has been the public policy exception of private international law:

[T]he practice of Western courts has produced a system of exceptions from the rules of conflict of laws in force in various countries because of the Soviet approach to property relations and the rights of the individual in the Soviet Union. These exceptions formulate, on the one hand, various aspects of the doctrine of public policy and, on the other, the position of Soviet and satellite laws in the general picture of the mutual interpenetration of the national laws of various other countries.[46]

Through the years the consistent response of the American courts to Communist confiscations has been to minimize the

[45] Grzybowski, "Public Policy and Soviet Law in the West after World War II," 4 Am. J. Comp. L. 365 (1955).
[46] Id. at 365.

local impact by whatever device was available whenever application of the foreign "law" would run counter to the authoritative policies of the forum. Ordinarily this could be accomplished by ruling in favor of American nationals whatever the circumstances. When no American national was involved and the contest was between foreign nationals or Soviet law was being asserted by an American national the orientation was less clear. On those few occasions the choice was difficult for American courts.

WESTERN EUROPEAN—NAZI SEIZURES

American foreign policy since 1900 toward the countries of Western Europe has consistently been one of respectful friendliness, ranging from highest regard for England through occasional exasperation with France to vague animosity toward Franco Spain. The American judicial attitude toward Civil Law in general has been respectful. For the most part the cases concerning seizures by these countries are unexceptionably predictable.

Who	What	When	Where	Whither	Why
Baglin (French monk) v. Cusenier (Amer. corp.)[47]	"Chartreux" trademark infringement in America	1910	Fed. Ct. in N.Y.	Baglin wins	Cusenier cannot claim Amer. trademarks because of extraterritoriality of French confiscation decree
Frenkel & Co. (Amer. corp.) v. L'Urbaine Fire Ins. Co. (Fr. corp.)[48]	Accounting on $20 million in premiums earned in U.S.	1929	N.Y. State Court	Frenkel & Co. wins	L'Urbaine not entitled to rely on French decree of World War I against Germans because of public policy against extraterritorial seizures
Banco de España (Sp. gov't bank) v. Fed. Reserve Bank (U.S. gov't bank)[49]	5 million ounces of Fr. silver seized by Spanish Republicans and sold to U.S. and on deposit in U.S. with defendant bank	1940	Fed. Ct. in N.Y.	Fed. Res. wins	Fed. Reserve Bank could rely on the validity of the Act of State of the Spanish Repub. Gov't
Union Shipping & Trading Co. (Amer. corp.) v. U.S.[50]	Damages for ship wrecked in Franec during World War I	1942	Fed. Ct. in N.Y.	Union Shipping & Trading wins	Union Shipping could rely on orders of French port officer because it was Act of State
Bollack (French nat'l) v. Société Generale (French corp.)[51]	$52,350 in securities located in N.Y. with defendant who cited French confiscatory law in defense	1942	N.Y. State Court	Bollack wins	Société Gen. cannot rely on French confiscation because violation of N.Y. public policy and it is a foreign penal law

Who	What	When	Where	Whither	Why
Netherlands v. Fed. Reserve Bank (U.S. gov't bank)	Bearer bonds deposited with defendant by Amer. blackmarketeer in violation of U.S. freeze statutes	1953	Fed. Ct. in N.Y.	Netherlands wins	Exile Dutch Gov't decree valid inside Nazi-occupied Holland because Act of State and it was conservatory seizure

47 Baglin v. Cusenier Co., 221 U.S. 580 (1910).
48 Frenkel & Co. v. L'Urbaine Fire Ins. Co., 226 N.Y.S. 322, 167 N.E. 430 (1929).
49 Banco de España v. Federal Reserve Bank, 114 F.2d 438 (1940).
50 Union Shipping & Trading Co. v. U.S., 127 F.2d 771 (CCA 2 1942).
51 Bollack v. Société Generale, 263 App. Div. 601 (1942).
52 Netherlands v. Federal Reserve Bank, 201 F.2d 455 (CCA 2, 1953).

The theme of protecting American nationals runs strong in these cases. In the *Frenkel & Co.* case, for example, the American plaintiff was the successor to a German partnership which had entered into an agency agreement with the defendant (a French corporation doing business also in New York) and under the agreement the German firm was entitled to commissions. During World War I France declared void all contracts between German and French nationals. The French defendant relied on this decree in refusing to pay the American plaintiff. The court said: "We think there is no principle of private or public international law that imposes on our courts a duty to enforce [this decree]. We would depart from our settled rule if we were to hold that either comity or public policy would require us to give effect to a confiscatory mandate of a foreign power against our own citizen."[53] And in the *Banco de España* case the court held for the American officials who were deposit agents for $2 million worth of confiscated silver purchased by the U.S. government from the Spanish Republicans, because: "Persons who dealt with the former Spanish government are entitled to rely upon the finality and legality of that government's acts, at least so far as concerns inquiry by the courts of this country."[54] The case of the *Netherlands v. Federal Reserve Bank* involved claims to securities held by the defendant as depositary. One Archidemes, an American national who purchased the securities on the black market in Switzerland and was caught by the U.S. government, claimed them against the state of Netherlands which relied on its wartime confiscation decree issued by the Dutch government in exile in England. Archidemes had no title, the court said, because he was not a holder in due course and was subject to federal exchange freeze orders. The court had a difficult time finding that the Netherlands decree had any force at all inside Nazi-occupied Holland. But once past that conceptual hurdle, the way was clear to hold that:

[53] Frenkel & Co. v. L'Urbaine Fire Ins. Co., *supra* note 48 at 432.
[54] Banco de España v. Federal Reserve Bank, *supra* note 49 at 444.

Since Decree A-1 does not conflict with any legitimate legislation or regulation of the occupant or with our own public policy, we see no reason why it should not be given effect in the present case. This conclusion received further support from the fact that, so far as appears, the claim of the Netherlands does not compete with any valid rights of United States residents.[55]

This case illustrates the conservative seizure theory whereby extraterritorial seizures are judicially recognized as valid by American courts because they approve of the motives of the seizing government and no local interests are jeopardized by so holding. That the United States and the legitimate government of Holland were jointly engaged in a war against the conquering Nazis at the time of the lawsuit amply explains the reason for this exception to the normal rule which would deny extraterritorial seizures regardless of the good motives of the seizing government.

The Nazi Seizures

The big anomaly resulting from this tendency to honor seizures by Western European nations concerned German seizures during the Second World War. American courts found themselves hoist by their own Act of State petard in the cases arising from the World War II Nazi confiscations of Jewish property under the infamous Nuremberg Laws, as this table shows:

[55] Netherlands v. Federal Reserve Bank, *supra* note 52 at 463.

Who	What	When	Where	Whither	Why
Steinfink (Ger. nat'l) v. North German Lloyd Steamship Co. (Ger. corp.)[56]	Return of $627 paid defendant for passage from Eng. in 1940	1938	N.Y. State Court	North German Steamship wins	North German can rely on German foreign exchange law to refuse to pay back the money
Holzer (Ger. Jew) v. Deutsche Reichsbahn-Gesellschaft (Ger. corp.)[57]	$600,000 damages for breach of employment contract in Germany	1938	N.Y. State Court	Deutsche Reichsbahn-Gesellschaft wins	Defendant can rely on German Nuremberg Law because of Act of State Doctrine
Werfel (Aust/Czech Jew) v. Zivnostanka Banka (Czech corp. now Ger. corp.)[58]	$5,848 deposited with defendant who now has money in Chase Nat'l Bank	1941	N.Y. State Court	Zivnostanka Banka wins	Defendant can rely on Nazi confiscation decrees because a part of foreign exchange regulations
Kleve (Ger. Jew) v. Basler Lebens-Versicherungs-Gesellschaft (Swiss corp.)[59]	Surrender values of policies seized in Germany; defendant's assets attached in N.Y.	1943	N.Y. State Court	Baslen Gesell. wins	Swiss company can rely on Nazi law because place of performance was Germany and Act of State Doctrine
Bernstein (Ger. Jew) v. Van-Heyghen Frère S. A. (Dutch corp.)[60]	Damages, profits and insurance proceeds from ship line seized in Germany; ins. proceeds attached in N.Y.	1943	Fed. Ct. in N.Y.	Van-Heyghen Frère S. A. wins	Act of State Doctrine

Who	What	When	Where	Whither	Why
Bernstein (Ger. Jew) v. N.V. Nederlandsche Amerikaansche Stoomvaart Maatschappij (Dutch corp.) [61]	$12.4 million damages and profits plus insurance proceeds and sale proceeds from ships seized in Germany and transferred to defendant	1954	Fed. Ct. in N.Y.	Bernstein wins (after State Dept. letter)	State Dept. letter permitting courts to inquire into Nazi confiscation laws and avoid Act of State Doctrine

[56] Steinfink v. North German Lloyd Steamship Co., 27 N.Y.S.2d 918 (1941).
[57] Holzer v. Deutsche Reichsbahn-Gesellschaft, 14 N.E.2d 798 (1938).
[58] Werfel v. Zivnostanka Banka, 23 N.Y.S.2d 1001, 38 N.E.2d 382 (1941).
[59] Kleve v. Basler Lebens-Versicherungs-Gesellschaft, 45 N.Y.S.2d 882 (1943).
[60] Bernstein v. Van-Heyghen Frère S.A., 163 F.2d 247 (CCA 2, 1947), cert. denied 332 U.S. 772 (1947).
[61] Bernstein v. N.V. Nederlandsche-Amerikansche Stoomvaart Maatshapij, 173 F.2d 71 (1949) modified on rehearing 210 F.2d 375 (1954). (Responding to State Dep't Letter).

The Jewish plaintiffs in each of these cases urged the invalidity of the Nazi Nuremberg Law confiscations because of the racial discrimination aspect but American courts hypocritically avoided this point. A rigidly doctrinaire version of the Act of State Doctrine served to uphold these Nazi confiscations. The judicial notion was that all foreign law must be recognized here, and the fact that this recognition served to implement vicious, discredited Nazi "law" was blissfully ignored.

The clearest statement of this rationalization appears in the *Holzer* case where the New York court was asked to strike down a defense based on the Nuremberg Laws, and the court replied: "Within its own territory every government is supreme and our courts are not competent to review its actions. We have so held, however objectionable we may consider the conduct of a foreign government."[62] Thereupon the Act of State formula was repeated, together with the statement from *Dougherty* that it was not against the public policy of New York to "hold nationals to the contracts which they have made in their own country to be performed there according to the laws of that country."[63] The *Kleve* case involved an even more gross situation. The Swiss insurance company had an office and assets in New York, but the plaintiffs' policies were "German" contracts. The Swiss company claimed the debt was discharged by coerced payment of the policy values to the Nazi government under the Nuremberg Laws. The American court agreed:

The governing law is no less controlling because it is bad law. The plaintiffs shift the point when they argue that our courts will not enforce foreign law contrary to our own public policy. This is not a case of enforcing German law but rather of necessarily recognizing the force of German law by applying it to the assets of these plaintiffs in this country but we cannot undo or set at naught what has been done by the German government with the assets of the parties in Germany. . . . Our courts have repeatedly

[62] Holzer v. Deutsche Reichsbahn-Gesellschaft, *supra* note 57 at 800.
[63] *Id.* at 800.

held, as a matter of necessity, that their judgment in such matters cannot be affected by the obnoxious character of the foreign law.[64]

The plaintiffs pointed out that they were not German nationals when the surrender values were "seized" and thus the German law should not apply to them, but the court stuck grimly to its quaint positivist notions.

The Bernstein Affair

The final judicial ignominy was registered in the *Bernstein* cases. Bernstein, a German Jew, owned two shipping lines. These were extorted from him by Nazi officials who had him turn them over to one Boeger in 1937. The ship *Gandia* was subsequently transferred to Van-Heyghen Frères Société Anonyme (a Belgian corporation) which let it out to the British on time charter. During the war the ship was sunk and the insurance proceeds were paid to another corporation which held them in New York as agent for Van-Heyghen. Bernstein was ransomed from Germany in 1939 and came to the United States where, in 1946 he attached the insurance proceeds and sued Van-Heyghen in a New York state court. The action was removed to the federal court which dismissed the complaint on the Recognition-Act of State formula, namely, the Nazi government having been duly recognized at the time of the seizures in the 1930s— their acts of state would be enforced by American courts forever after. This was affirmed on appeal—result and reason —because the Act of State Doctrine meant that "no court will exercise its jurisdiction to adjudicate the validity of the official acts of another state."[65] But Bernstein had another shipping line left. His Red Star Line had been seized and then transferred to N. V. Nederlandsche-Amerikaansche

[64] Kleve v. Basler Lebens-Versicherungs-Gesellschaft, *supra* note 59 at 887.
[65] Bernstein v. Van-Heyghen Frère S.A., *supra* note 60. (Because of possible undesirable interference with executive foreign relations activities.)

70

Stoomvaart-Maatschapij (Holland-American) upon inadequate consideration and with notice to Holland-American of the circumstances. Bernstein sued Holland-American in a federal court in New York despite losing his first case. The trial court dismissed the action because of the first *Bernstein* case, and this was also affirmed in 1949 by the Second Circuit Court of Appeals.[66] This result was too outrageous for even the normally reticent State Department, however, and on April 27, 1949, two months after the second *Bernstein* case had been affirmed, the State Department released to the press a celebrated letter unleashing the American courts:

> This government has consistently opposed the forcible acts of dispossession of a discriminatory and confiscatory nature practiced by the Germans on the countries or peoples subject to their controls. . . . The policy of the Executive, with respect to claims asserted in the United States for the restitution of identifiable property (or compensation in lieu thereof) lost through force, coercion, or duress as a result of Nazi persecution in Germany, is to relieve American courts from any restraint upon the exercise of their jurisdiction to pass on the validity of the acts of Nazi officials.[67]

Upon publication of this official statement the Second Circuit Court of Appeals amended its mandate in the case to permit Bernstein to recover. Thus the so-called Bernstein Exception to the Act of State Doctrine was formulated: American courts are foreclosed by the Act of State Doctrine from inquiry into the validity of foreign seizures of property because of possible interference with the Executive Branch until and unless the State Department notifies the court otherwise concerning a specific case.

From this history of judicial involvement in Communist and Nazi seizures derive two basic ideas. The Soviet seizure cases manifest a settled judicial policy to thwart

[66] Bernstein v. N.V. Nederlandsche-Amerikansche Stoomvaart Maatshapij, *supra* note 61.
[67] State Department Press Release 296, April 27, 20 State Dep't Bull 592 (1949).

71

Communist attempts extraterritorially to impose their "law" on local assets, a policy broken only rarely by extreme solicitation for the interests of American nationals, or, as in the *Pink* case, by an exception to strict territoriality theory when the Executive, acting on the strength of its constitutional authority to conduct foreign affairs, by means of a treaty (or its equivalent) dictates otherwise. From the Nazi seizures came the so-called Bernstein Exception to the Act of State Doctrine. Although never officially sanctioned by the United States Supreme Court, the judicial deference to the State Department paid by the Second Circuit Court of Appeals was thought to be authoritative and indicated the State Department tail wagged the judicial dog. The Bernstein Exception signified the rising strength of the State Department in private litigation concerning foreign seizures of private property. Together with the old South American seizure cases establishing the Act of State Doctrine, it formed a bewildering pattern of law concerning the American judicial response to foreign seizures of private property.

None of these seizure cases presented to the Supreme Court clear-cut instances of foreign seizures of American-owned assets located overseas in clear violation of well-settled international law principles. The *Sabbatino* case finally presented to the Supreme Court a fact situation involving a foreign seizure of American-owned movables alleged to be in violation of international law which incorporated all three now-familiar stress factors: 1) a "Communist" seizure, 2) by a South American government, 3) in which the State Department manifested disapproval of judicial inquiry into the merits.

The result was another example that "all compromises are odious."

4

THE *SABBATINO* CASE

*T*HE UNITED STATES Department of State had never been directly involved in a foreign seizure case before the United States Supreme Court prior to the *Sabbatino* case in 1963. Its presence in that case was important to the decision; perhaps it was actually determinative. This importance appears clearly from the history of the development of the Act of State Doctrine, the *Pink* case decision in 1942, and—most significantly—from the intervention by the State Department in the second *Bernstein* case in 1954 by issuance of its official letter. Genuine irony resides in the fact that the "unleashing" of American courts in 1954 by the Department of State nearly culminated in shackling them to a role of utter subserviency to the Department of State in 1964. How this occurred makes a fascinating story.

Supreme Court decisions implementing national foreign policies in *Underhill, American Banana, Ricaud* and *Oetjen* had created the Act of State Doctrine by 1920 and had established as the "law of the land" the "rule for decision" principle concerning the validity of foreign seizures. None of these early cases involved foreign seizures in violation of international law, nor was it made clear whether federal or state law controlled. The Supreme Court in the *Pink* case in 1942 announced that judicial determination of ownership interests in local movables seized by foreign acts of state was a matter to be decided in light of national foreign policy as spelled out by the Executive branch—especially when the Executive branch was claiming the property under an Executive agreement. Moreover, the Supreme Court held that this national policy would not be thwarted by conflicting state policy for the same reasons which underpinned the Act of State Doctrine. The Act of State Doctrine appeared even more clearly to be the law of the land. The Bernstein affair culminated in a holding by Judge Learned Hand, speaking for the Second Circuit Court of Appeals, that the validity of Nazi seizures of Jewish properties under the infamous Nuremberg Laws could not be invalidated by an American court in 1953 because of a possible conflict between a judicial ruling and the conduct by the Executive branch of postwar administrative activities in Western Europe. The State Department letter, issued after the judicial ruling had been made but before it became final, served to notify the federal court that the Executive branch had no objections to judicial determination of legal claims concerning such privately owned movables. This unleashed the Second Circuit Court of Appeals, and it thereupon changed its ruling and returned the ship line to its rightful owner. The sum and substance of the second Bernstein affair apparently was that in the absence of a State Department release, the federal judiciary was bound by the Act of State Doctrine which prohibited review of foreign seizures. Still none of these cases had clearly involved foreign seizures in violation of international law because Bernstein was a German citizen at the time of the seizure.

International law had also been the law of the land for a long time. This had been true for so long that "the memory of man runneth not to the contrary" because the proposition came to this country via the Common Law of England. The Federalist Papers, the debates in conjunction with the constitutional convention, and the text of the Constitution itself all bear evidence of the fact. Two years after adoption of the Constitution Chief Justice Jay in *Chisholm v. Georgia* noted that even before the date of the Constitution "the United States had, by taking a place among the nations of the earth, become amenable to the law of nations."[1] Only four years after adoption of the Constitution in the celebrated case of *Ware v. Hylton* the Supreme Court stated that upon achieving its independence the United States was "bound to receive the law of nations in its modern state of purity and refinement."[2] Chief Justice Marshall stated explicitly in the *Nereide* case in 1815 that without an act of Congress to the contrary, "the Court is bound by the law of nations which is part of the law of the land."[3] This statement was made only three years after his decision in *The Schooner Exchange* case which was one of our earliest seizure cases. But the most popular statement of this rule of law is the formulation by Justice Gray in *The Paquete Habana* case in 1900: "International law is part of our law and must be ascertained and administered by the courts of justice of appropriate jurisdiction, as often as questions of right depending upon them are duly presented for their determination."[4] A great number of other cases also found the United States Supreme Court invoking the general principle that the law of nations was part of the law of the land.

[1] 2 Dall. 419, 474 (1793).
[2] 3 Dall. 199, 281 (1796).
[3] 9 Cranch 388, 423 (1815).
[4] The Paquete Habana, 175 U.S. 677 (1900).

Proof that this was not just judicial bombast arises from the many applications of particular rules of international law in specific situations. The range of the subjects thus covered is broad: 1) federal crimes (before federal criminal law became statutory), 2) maritime cases, 3) acquisition and control of territory cases, 4) resolution of boundary disputes, 5) the effect of transfers of territory on private rights, 6) nationality questions, 7) sovereign immunity cases, 8) treaty cases, 9) cases involving the international law of war, and 10) instances involving the law of neutrality. International law was clearly not an ignored part of the law of the land.

Potential conflict between these two equally well-established laws of the land, the Law of Nations and the Act of State Doctrine, never materialized. Throughout their long histories no case in the Supreme Court clearly presented an instance of a foreign seizure in violation of international law. Thus the potential conflict between these two principles of law could be rationalized several ways: 1) the Act of State Doctrine is so strong an inhibition on the American judiciary that it overrides both the general duty of a court to decide all proper cases brought before it and the specific obligation to apply international law when the case involves a violation thereof, and thus the Doctrine would be dogmatically applied; 2) the Act of State Doctrine would be dogmatically applied unless the State Department unleashed the judiciary by means of a specific official letter; 3) the Act of State Doctrine is qualified by an exception which permits judicial review in cases concerning foreign seizures in violation of international law; or 4) the Act of State Doctrine is qualified by an international law exception unless the State Department shackles the judiciary by means of a reverse Bernstein letter, namely, by advising the court that the Executive branch objects on grounds of possible interference with its conduct of foreign affairs.

Proposition number one we will call the Doctrinaire version, number two the Department of State version, number three the International Law Association version, and number four the Association of the Bar of New York City version. They are named for the parties advocating them before the United States Supreme Court in the *Sabbatino* case.

Thus the matter stood in 1960.

PRECIPITATING EVENTS

The institution, progress, and ultimate success of the Revolution of July 26 in Cuba during the years 1957-1959 is familiar history. Following the revolution came the "Bay of Pigs" affair, which was an attempted counter-revolutionary invasion of the island by Cuban exiles in which the United States government played an indeterminate part. Shortly thereafter, the United States Congress voted to extend to the President authority to alter the sugar quota previously established for Cuba under the Sugar Act of 1948. The Castro government on July 6, 1960, responded by enacting Law 851, which authorized compulsory expropriation of American-owned property whenever deemed "advisable in order to defend the national interests." The following day, on July 7, 1960, the President of the United States reduced the Cuba sugar quota.

General Sugar Estates, Inc., was a wholly owned Cuban subsidiary of Compañía Azucarera Vertientes-Camaguey de Cuba (CAV), a Cuban corporation ninety percent owned by American citizens. CAV had contracted during February and July, 1960, to sell a quantity of sugar to Farr, Whitlock & Co., a partnership of brokers in New York City. Some 22,000 bags of Cuban sugar were loaded onto a German ship situated offshore from the Cuban port of Jucaro during the weekend of August 6-9, pursuant to the contract.

During that same weekend Fidel Castro promulgated a "joint resolution," on August 6, 1960, under Law 851, nationalizing American-owned enterprises located in Cuba, especially CAV, and designating a Cuban bank as the agent for receiving the assets. Permission of the Cuban government was required by the Act before any ship in Cuban waters could sail. This provided the leverage whereby Farr, Whitlock was forced to enter into substituted contracts of sale in which Banco para el Comercio Exterior de Cuba, the official designee, purported to transfer the sugar to the New York firm on August 11, 1960, for $175,250.69. Only then was the German ship allowed to depart and the sugar thereafter moved into international trade channels. The contracts were assigned to Banco Nacional de Cuba (Banco Nacional) who subsequently sent the shipping documents with sight draft attached to a French bank located in New York City (Société Generale) for collection. The documents and draft were presented to Farr, Whitlock who eventually collected the sale proceeds from the customer. But because of the conflicting claims by Banco Nacional and Sabbatino, who had been appointed by a New York state court Receiver for CAV assets located in New York,[5] Farr, Whitlock refused to remit the proceeds to the French bank.

Banco Nacional commenced a suit in federal court in New York claiming conversion of the proceeds by Farr, Whitlock. Sabbatino, the most-interested party, asserted that the foreign law under which Banco Nacional was claiming "title" to the money was invalid for a variety of reasons, the principal one being that the seizure was in violation of international law. The Cuban bank in rejoinder sought to prevent judicial inquiry into the validity of the Cuban decree under any criterion by invoking the Act of State Doctrine.

THE LOWER COURT DECISIONS

The trial court held in favor of the defendants. After holding that the Federal District Court had jurisdiction over the person of Sabbatino, the appointed Receiver, and the

[5] Sabbatino had previously been appointed Temporary Receiver of CAV's New York assets under a state statute expressly designed for such purposes. New York Civil Practice Act § 977-b.

proceeds of the sale, the Court ruled on the merits and rejected several minor contentions by the defendants. The defendants' major claim asserted the unenforceability of the Cuban decree in this country for several reasons. The court rejected most of these reasons except the "crucial question . . . whether this court can examine the validity of the Cuban act under international law and refuse recognition . . . if it is in violation of international law," and held that in the circumstances of the present action the law of the forum would not enforce the Cuban decree if it violated international law.[6]

Banco Nacional de Cuba appealed to the Second Circuit Court of Appeals, and the appellate court affirmed the lower court award in favor of Sabbatino and Farr, Whitlock.[7] The CCA opinion followed the District Court reasoning closely and after reciting the facts it affirmed the ruling that the District Court had jurisdiction over both Sabbatino and the money. Then the discussion on the merits noted:

The policies and theories underlying this doctrine of judicial abnegation seem to be these: The desire by the judiciary to avoid possible conflict with or embarrassment to the executive and legislative branches of our Government in our dealings with foreign nations . . . a positivistic concept of territorial sovereignty . . . and a fear of hampering international trade by rendering titles insecure. . . . It has also been suggested that the remoteness of American courts from the circumstances surrounding the making of the foreign decree and the provincial attitude taken by most municipal courts make American courts unsuitable tribunals for judging the validity of acts committed by foreign sovereigns within their territorial limits.

The Circuit Court of Appeals then noted an exception to the Act of State Doctrine which arises when the executive branch of the U.S. government does not oppose inquiry into the legality of a foreign act of state. The court observed

[6] Banco Nacional de Cuba v. Sabbatino, 193 F. Supp. 275 (U.S.D.C.S.D.N.Y., 1961).
[7] Banco Nacional de Cuba v. Sabbatino, 307 F.2d 845 (CCA 2, 1962).

that a diplomatic note had been delivered to Cuba on this matter, and that State Department letters declining comment on judicial inquiry had recently gone to the lower court in this case and to several other federal courts in similar cases involving Cuban seizures. This cleared the way for adoption of defendant's major contention that Banco Nacional de Cuba had a defective title under international law and thus was not entitled to recover the sale proceeds.

THE SUPREME COURT DECISION

Banco Nacional de Cuba thereupon filed a petition for certiorari in the United States Supreme Court which was subsequently granted.[8] By this time the case had attracted considerable attention, and an impressive array of interested parties was lined up on each side of the lawsuit.

The petitioner in the case on appeal to the United States Supreme Court was Banco Nacional de Cuba, who contended for proposition number one, the Doctrinaire version of Act of State, and urged reversal of the lower court decisions. The Cubans attracted some strange bedfellows. Also urging reversal was the United States Department of Justice on behalf of the Department of State speaking as amicus curiae. The Department of Justice urged proposition number two—the Department of State version—that no exception to the Act of State Doctrine should be approved other than the Bernstein Exception, and contended that the Judiciary had not been "unleashed" by the Department of State despite the noncommittal letters issued in the case. Essentially, the Department of State maintained it had not yet spoken within the meaning of the Bernstein rule.

On the opposite side of the lawsuit was a formidable group. The respondents Farr, Whitlock and cav relied

---

[8] Certiorari was granted by the United States Supreme Court on February 18, 1963, 372 U.S. 905 (1963), and after oral argument on October 22 and 23, 32 U.S. Law Week 3157 (1963), the Court rendered its decision on March 23, 1964, 84 Sup. Ct. 923 (1964), reversing the judgment.

upon the two lower federal court rulings in their favor which substantially embodied proposition number three that the Act of State Doctrine was qualified by an exception where seizures in violation of international law were involved. They were joined in this contention by the Executive Committee of the American Branch of the International Law Association which filed its brief amicus curiae urging proposition number three. Sugar industry spokesmen supported the respondents with a brief amicus curiae. The Committee on International Law of the Association of the Bar of New York City filed its brief urging proposition number four that the Act of State Doctrine was qualified by an exception in cases of seizures violating international law unless the Department of State objected. Finally, the American Bar Association Section of International and Comparative Law urged in its brief amicus curiae that the taking was in violation of international law and assumed that the Act of State Doctrine was inapplicable in the case.

Acting Secretary of State Christian Herter took the public, official position at the time of enactment of Law 851 in 1960 that it was "manifestly in violation of these principles of international law which have long been accepted by the free countries of the West . . . in its essence (the law is) discriminatory, arbitrary and confiscatory." Consistent with this position and its settled procedures in such cases, the Department of State twice stated in writing that it was taking no legal position on the case while it was in the lower courts. Abram Chayes, Legal Adviser to the Department of State, answered an inquiry concerning the legal position of the Department by a letter on October 18, 1961, in which he stated:

The Department of State has not, in the Bahia de Nipe case [involving other Cuban seizures] or elsewhere, done anything inconsistent with the position taken on the Cuban nationalization by Secretary Herter. Whether or not these nationalizations will in the future be given effect in the United States is, of course, for the courts to determine. Since the Sabbatino case and other similar cases are at present before the courts, any comments on this question by the Department of State would be out of place at this time.[9]

A similar letter from George Ball, Under Secretary for Economic Affairs, on November 14, 1961, was even more unequivocal on this point, for Mr. Ball expressly declined to comment at all.

While the *Sabbatino* case was before the lower federal courts the United States froze all Cuban assets in this country, established a limited trade embargo against the island, forced the Castro Government to remove its offensive missile emplacements and return the hardware to Russia, and, finally, broke off diplomatic relations with Cuba in 1963. The familiar succession of events included our vote and influence in the actions of the Organization of American States invoking sanctions against the Castro Government and the Cuban counterblow of turning off the water at Guantanamo Naval Base. Through it all the Department of State hewed to the national foreign policy line that the Cuban seizures were violations of international law to be condemned by all civilized nations and the proper subject for the imposition of domestic, national, and international sanctions. Presumably this was the view of the entire Executive Branch of our government. But when the United States Supreme Court invited the views of the Solicitor General of the United States, some alchemy in the decision-making processes within the Department of State wrought a wondrous clarification of its position.

The Department of Justice, speaking through Assistant Attorney General Nicholas deB. Katzenbach and representing the Department of State, submitted a brief amicus curiae and argued orally that 1) There was no Bernstein expression from the Department of State which would permit judicial inquiry under that exception to the Act of State Doctrine; 2) Executive silence on the point is not equivalent to executive approval of judicial inquiry and 3) the "balance of

[9] Banco Nacional de Cuba v. Sabbatino, 84 Sup. Ct. 923, 936 n. 19 (1964).

considerations strongly favors the retention of the traditional [Act of State] doctrine" and the "international law exception" should not be adopted.

The ambiguity in the Department's previous position, said the United States Supreme Court, "is now removed by the position which the Executive has taken in this Court on the Act of State claim." Ostensibly declining to utilize the Bernstein rationalization urged by the Department of State, namely, that the Act of State Doctrine applied until and unless specifically, clearly, and officially lifted by a suggestion to that effect from the Department, the Court thereupon proceeded nevertheless to ascribe to the Department's formal and official posture crucially pragmatic legal consequences. Executive objection to Judicial inquiry, manifested by the Department of State's brief and argument, apparently sufficed to shift the whole burden of the appeal from the Cuban bank onto Sabbatino, Farr, Whitlock, and CAV, because the Court stated:

The outcome of this case, therefore, turns upon whether any of the contentions urged by respondents against application of the Act of State Doctrine in the premises is acceptable: (1) That the doctrine does not apply to acts of state which violate international law, as is claimed to be the case here; (2) that the doctrine is inapplicable unless the Executive specifically interposes it in a particular case; and (3) that in any event, the doctrine may not be invoked by a foreign government plaintiff in our courts.[10]

This approach reverses the one ordinarily taken, since the burden of persuading the Court (or the risk of non-persuasion) normally is on the party bringing the appeal who has lost his case below and seeks reversal. Generally speaking, the appellant loses on his appeal unless he can persuade the upper court that the lower court ruling was erroneous as a matter of law. But in the passage quoted above the Court put that risk on the respondents, who had won in both lower courts.

The Act of State Doctrine, said the Court, rests not on

[10] *Id.* at 938.

"the inherent nature of sovereign authority" nor on "some principle of international law," nor does the United States Constitution require it because nothing in that document "irrevocably remove(s) from the judiciary the capacity" to sit in judgment on foreign acts of state. The true foundation of the Doctrine is the separation of powers principle in the Constitution: "The doctrine as formulated in past decisions expresses the strong sense of the Judicial Branch that its engagement in the task of passing on the validity of foreign acts of state may hinder rather than further this country's pursuit of goals both for itself and for the community of nations as a whole in the international sphere."[11] Admitting that there was little or no direct precedent to support the precise proposition urged by the Cuban bank and the State Department—namely—that the Doctrine applied even to seizures in violation of international law, because no previous decision had treated the precise problem, Mr. Justice Harlan concluded that nevertheless "we can assume" the same principles apply to all seizures. The Court thereupon reasoned that since application of the Act of State Doctrine is neither compelled nor prohibited by either international law or the United States Constitution, the whole question becomes one of balancing the relevant considerations to "the proper distribution of functions between the judicial and political branches" concerning this particular aspect of foreign affairs. This Frankfurterian approach is justified by Mr. Justice Harlan in the following passage which states the "major premise" of the court:

It should be apparent that the greater the degree of codification or consensus concerning a particular area of international law, the more appropriate it is for the judiciary to render decisions regarding it, since the courts can then focus on the application of an agreed principle to circumstances of fact, rather than on the sensitive task of establishing a principle not inconsistent with the national interest or with international justice.[12]

[11] *Ibid.*
[12] *Id.* at 940.

The "minor premise" in the syllogism of the Court's argument is that there is no appreciable international consensus concerning expropriations because the Western nations and Communist countries disagree on whether compensation must be paid; the "newly independent and underdeveloped countries" disagree with traditional international law on whether the property of an alien should be given special protection over the property of nationals; the capital importing and capital exporting states have divergent national interests in the matter; and, the capitalist countries and socialist countries disagree on the relative importance of private property in general. These points seem critically important, for the Court notes:

There are few if any issues in international law today on which opinion seems to be so divided as the limitations on a State's power to expropriate the property of aliens. . . . It is difficult to imagine the courts of this country embarking on adjudication in an area which touches more sensitively the practical and ideological goals of the various members of the community of nations.[13]

From these assumptions by the Court flowed the precise holding in the case which purported to be based on the balance of "relevant considerations" in this particular litigation:

Therefore, rather than laying down or reaffirming an inflexible and all-encompassing rule in this case, we decide only that the Judicial Branch will not examine the validity of a taking of property within its own territory by a foreign sovereign government, extant and recognized by this country at the time of suit, in the absence of a treaty or other unambiguous agreement regarding controlling legal principles, even if the complaint alleges that the taking violated customary international law.[14]

This holding amounts to automatic application of the classic Act of State Doctrine and thus was a clear selection by the Court of proposition number one—the Doctrinaire version.

[13] *Ibid.*
[14] *Ibid.*

JUSTICE WHITE'S DISSENT

A strong dissenting opinion was written by Mr. Justice White. Like a man fervently trying to prove a negative proposition—a practically impossible task under the best circumstances—he drew heavily from the contentions of the respondents and the International Law Association in urging proposition number three and advocating affirmance of the lower court decisions. His analysis of the legal position taken by the State Department differs from that of the Court which treated it as an unambiguous objection to judicial inquiry. Mr. Justice White interpreted the stance as still ambiguous:

> As I understand it, the executive has not yet said that adjudication in this case would impede his functions in the premises; rather it has asked us to adopt a rule of law foreclosing inquiry into the subject unless the executive affirmatively allows the courts to adjudicate on the merits. . . . The position of the Executive Branch of the Government charged with foreign affairs with respect to this case is not entirely clear. As I see it no specific objection by the Secretary of State to examination of the validity of Cuba's law has been interposed at any stage in these proceedings. . . . If my view had prevailed I would have stayed further resolution of the issues in this Court to afford the Department of State reasonable time to clarify its views in light of the opinion. In the absence of a specific objection to an examination of the validity of Cuba's law under international law, I would have proceeded to determine the issue and resolve this litigation on the merits.[15]

But his view did not prevail despite the fact that his line of reasoning parallels, crosses, and dashes far ahead of the plodding analysis made by the Court.

He agreed with the majority that the Act of State Doctrine is neither a rule of international law nor compelled by the Constitution and that it is the expression of a generally wise judicial policy which "reflects an effort to maintain a certain stability and predictability in transna-

[15] *Id.* at 962.

86

tional transactions, to avoid friction between nations, to encourage settlement of these disputes through diplomatic means and to avoid interference with the executive control of foreign relations."[16] Also in agreement with the majority, he found himself convinced that the matter was not foreclosed by prior rulings, and, moreover, that the many cases in which the Court has struggled with foreign seizure problems amply "demonstrate that our courts have never been bound to pay unlimited deference to foreign acts of state." But further than this he could not go with the Court.

White took a considerably broader view of the entire matter than did the majority, and his analysis reaches incalculably further than that of the majority and its narrow preoccupation with legal technicalities. Moreover, the structure of his reasoning gives weight to matters altogether ignored by the Court. White begins at a point never reached by the Court:

I start with what I thought to be unassailable propositions: that our courts are obliged to determine controversies on their merits, in accordance with the applicable law; and that part of the law American courts are bound to administer is international law. . . . Principles of international law have been applied in our courts to resolve controversies not merely because they provide a convenient rule for decision but because they represent a consensus among civilized nations on the proper ordering of relations between nations and the citizens thereof. Fundamental fairness to litigants as well as the interest in stability of relationships and preservation of reasonable expectations call for their application whenever international law is controlling in a case or controversy.[17]

Sketching briefly the precedent for these assertions, he proceeded to detail the particular aspects of this case which already involve application of the rules of international law which the Court apparently accepts. He noted that the case already involves the necessity for choosing which national law is applicable to the transaction because of the inter-

16 *Id.* at 950.
17 *Id.* at 952.

national law concept of territorial sovereignty generating the situs rule of conflicts of law which dictates that Cuban law governs the "title" question; moreover, the international law rules on territorial boundaries already have been utilized to decide that the ship was within Cuban waters at the time of the "seizure," and "the law merchant common to civilized countries" has been applied to determine the legal effect of the seizure on the documentary exchange in New York. Having swallowed all that, White charges that the Court then lightly:

[D]ispenses with its obligation to resolve controversies in accordance with "international justice" and the "national interest" by assuming and declaring that there are no areas of agreement between nations in respect to expropriations. There may not be, but without critical examination . . . I would not conclude that a confiscatory taking which discriminates against nationals of another country to retaliate against the government of that country falls within that area of issues in international law "on which opinion seems to be so divided." Nor would I assume, as the ironclad rule of the Court necessarily implies, that there is not likely to be a consensus among nations in this area, as for example upon the illegality of discriminatory takings of alien property based upon race, religion or nationality. But most of all I would not declare that even if there were a clear consensus in the international community, the courts must close their eyes to a lawless act and validate the transgression by rendering judgment for the foreign state at its own request. . . . I cannot so cavalierly ignore the obligations of a court to dispense justice to the litigants before it.[18]

And this is the heart of his position to which he returns time after time throughout the remainder of his opinion: The primary social duty of a court is to decide cases properly brought before it by application of rules of law, including, in the case of American courts, international law when applicable, and the Doctrinaire version of the Act of State Doctrine forestalls any possibility for discharge of this duty by prohibiting any inquiry into the validity of foreign seizures under any possible legal standards.

[18] *Id.* at 954.

ANALYTICAL COMPARISON OF THE
MAJORITY AND MINORITY OPINIONS

Stripped to the bare bones of the matter, the difference between the majority position embodied in Mr. Justice Harlan's opinion and the dissent filed by Mr. Justice White is not very great at first glance. The essential action of the Court was reversal of the lower court decision in favor of Farr, Whitlock, Sabbatino, and CAV and a remand of the case to the lower court to be finally determined in favor of Banco Nacional de Cuba in light of the ruling that the validity of the Cuban seizure could not be inquired into because of the Act of State Doctrine. The upshot of the case was that the Cuban bank was entitled to the $175,250.69. The majority and dissenting opinions can be read to disagree merely on a rather minor point, namely, whether the State Department had clearly objected to judicial review in this specific case. Harlan thought it had, and White was not sure and would have stayed the proceedings to find out. Close study of the opinions, however, discloses that they were intellectually far apart on the major issues:

MAJORITY—[Respondent's] basic contention is that United States courts could make a significant contribution to the growth of international law, a contribution whose importance, it is said, would be magnified by the relative paucity of decisional law by international bodies. But given the fluidity of present world conditions, the effectiveness of such a patchwork approach towards the formulation of an acceptable body of law concerning state responsibility for expropriations is, to say the least, highly conjectural. Moreover, it rests upon the sanguine presupposition that the decisions of the courts of the world's major capital exporting country and principal exponent of the free-enterprise system would be accepted as disinterested expressions of sound legal principle by those adhering to widely different ideologies.[19]

THE EMBARRASSMENT

MAJORITY—Piecemeal dispositions of this sort (by courts) involving the probability of affront to another state could seriously interfere with negotiations being carried on by the Executive Branch. . . . If the Executive Branch has undertaken negotiations with an expropriating country, but has refrained from claims of violation of the law of nations, a determination to that effect by a court might be regarded as a serious insult, while a finding of compliance with international law would greatly strengthen the bargaining hand of the other State with consequent detriment to American interests . . . even if the State Department has proclaimed the impropriety of the expropriation, the stamp of approval of its view by a judicial tribunal, however impartial, might increase any affront . . . considerably more serious and far-reaching consequences would flow from a judicial finding that international law standards had been met if that determination flew in the face of a State Department proclamation to the contrary. . . . Respondents contend that, even if there is not agreement regarding general standards for determining the validity of expropriations, the alleged combination of retaliation,

[19] Id. at 942-44.

INTERNATIONAL LAW

DISSENT—Although a state may reasonably expect that the validity of its laws operating on property within its jurisdiction will not be defined by local notions of public policy of numerous other states . . . it cannot with impunity ignore the rules governing the conduct of all nations and expect that other nations and tribunals will view their acts as within the permissible scope of territorial sovereignty. Contrariwise, to refuse inquiry into the question of whether norms of international community have been contravened would seem to deny the existence or purport of such norms, a view that seems inconsistent with the role of international law in ordering the relations between nations. Finally, the impartial application of international law would not only be an affirmation of the existence and binding effect of international rules of order, but also a refutation of the notion that this body of law consists of no more than the divergent and parochial views of the capital importing and exporting nations, the socialist and free-enterprise nations.[20]

OF THE EXECUTIVE

DISSENT—The Court is moved by the spectre of another possibility . . . founded on the supposed impact of a judicial decision on diplomatic relations. . . . I fail to see how greater embarrassment flows from saying that the foreign act does not violate clear and widely accepted principles of international law than from saying as the Court does, that nonexamination and validation is required because there are no widely accepted principles to which to subject the foreign act . . . I would think that an adjudication by this Court that the foreign act to which the executive is protesting and attempting to secure relief for American citizens, is valid and beyond question enforcible in the courts of the United States would indeed prove embarrassing to the Executive Branch of our Government in many situations, much more so than a declaration of invalidity or a refusal to adjudicate the controversy at all. . . . The Court notes that "adverse domestic consequences might flow from an official stand," by which I take it to mean that it might be politically embarrassing on the domestic front for the Department of State to interpose an objection in a particular case . . . but an official stand is what

[20] *Id.* at 955-57.

discrimination, and inadequate compensation makes it patently clear that this particular expropriation was in violation of international law. If this view is accurate, it would still be unwise for the courts so to determine. Such a decision now would require the drawing of more difficult lines in subsequent cases and these would involve the possibility of conflict with the Executive view. Even if the courts avoided this course, either by presuming the validity of an act of state whenever the international law standard was thought unclear or by following the State Department declaration in such a situation, the very expressions of judicial uncertainty might prove embarrassing to the Executive Branch.[21]

JUDICIAL

MAJORITY—Judicial determination of invalidity of title can . . . have only an occasional impact . . . [and] be likely to give offence to the expropriating country . . . such a patchwork approach towards the formulation of an acceptable body of law concerning state responsibility for expropriations is, to say the least, highly conjectural . . . the deterrent effect of court invalidations would not ordinarily be great . . . any country willing to brave . . . these consequences [embargo, freezing of assets and lack of foreign capital] is unlikely to be deterred by sporadic judicial decisions . . . if the political branches are unwilling to exercise their ample powers to effect compensation, this reflects a judgment of the national interest which the judiciary would be ill advised to undermine indirectly.[22]

THE BIG

MAJORITY—However offensive to the public policy of this country and its constituent states an expropriation of this kind may be we conclude that both the national interest and progress towards the goal of establishing the rule of law among nations are best served by maintaining intact the act of state doctrine in this realm of its application.[23]

[21] *Id.* at 942-43.
[22] *Id.* at 942.
[23] *Id.* at 944.

the Department must take under the so-called Bernstein exception . . . it is not fair to allow the fate of a litigant to turn on the possible political embarrassment of the Department of State and it is not this Court's role to encourage or require nonexamination by bottoming a rule of law on the domestic public relations of the Department of State. . . . These speculations, founded on the supposed impact of a judicial decision on diplomatic relations, seem contrary to the Court's view of the arsenal of weapons possessed by this country to . . . secure foreign investment . . . [its] ample powers to effect compensation, and wholly inconsistent with its view of the limited competence and knowledge of the judiciary in the area of foreign affairs and diplomacy.[24]

INEFFECTIVENESS

DISSENT—. . . [States] cannot with impunity ignore the rules governing the conduct of all nations and expect that other nations and tribunals will view their acts as within the permissible scope of territorial sovereignty . . . [the majority position] would apply to any other problem arising from transactions that cross state lines . . . the achievement of a minimum amount of stability and predictability in international commercial transactions is not assured by a rule of non-reviewability which permits any act of a foreign state, regardless of its validity under international law, to pass muster in the courts of other states . . . [diplomatic relief] may be more often illusory than real . . . [particularly here] where no one has argued that CAV can obtain relief in the courts of Cuba.[25]

PICTURE

DISSENT—No other civilized country has found such a rigid rule necessary for the survival of the executive branch of its government, the executive of no other government seems to require such insulation from international law adjudications in its courts; and no other judiciary is apparently so incompetent to ascertain and apply international law.[26]

[24] *Id.* at 958-61.
[25] *Id.* at 955-56.
[26] *Id.* at 946.

The majority opinion is expressly grounded on a desire to preclude the possible application of narrow, parochial views by the American judiciary in matters having to do with foreign relations. The Act of State Doctrine itself is a pure expression of American parochialism when it is formulated to amount to a "flat rule of no inquiry" under any seizure circumstances. And the Court makes its argument in favor of the Doctrinaire version by use of the most narrow and parochial views of all, namely, that international law should come to American courts full grown, clear-cut, well-settled, and fully accepted by all other nations of the globe in order that our courts need only "focus on the application of an agreed principle to circumstances of fact rather than on the sensitive task of establishing a principle not inconsistent with the national interest or with international justice." This—as Mr. Justice White caustically notes—"is tantamount to a declaration excusing this Court from any future consequential role in the clarification and application of international law . . . [and] ignores the historic role which this Court and other American courts have played in applying and maintaining principles of international law."

A narrower and more outdated view of the judicial process in general and the processes of international law in particular cannot be imagined than that projected by the Court. Precisely how a global consensus on the international law of expropriations, or on any other point for that matter, will come into existence without the rational process of decision-making by responsible national agencies is left mercilessly vague in the majority opinion. Nevertheless, it is a reasonable inference from the majority opinion that the mystic processes of international diplomacy are thought to be the only legitimate source of "international law," properly so called. Even the authoritative writings of lifelong international law scholars is downgraded and ignored in the majority opinion. It is as plain as the positivist nose on the face of the Court's opinion that the United States Supreme

Court doubts both the existence and utility of international law for deciding other than rubberstamp cases.

The key assumption in the Court's line of reasoning is that there is absolutely no international consensus on the subject of expropriations, and thus American courts should not get into the matter at all. The broad sweep of this syllogism is limited somewhat by a laconic footnote afterthought that "this decision in no way intimates that the courts of this country are broadly foreclosed from considering questions of international law." Nevertheless, the clear implication remains that the Court believes there is no fundamental international agreement whatsoever concerning expropriations, an assertion which Mr. Justice White answers in successive footnote ripostes:

It strains credulity to accept the proposition that newly emerging nations or their spokesmen denounce all rules of state responsibility, reject international law in regard to foreign nationals generally, rather than reject the traditional rule of international law requiring prompt, adequate, and effective compensation. * * * There is another implication in the Court's opinion: the act of state doctrine applies to all expropriations, not only because of the lack of a consensus among nations on any standards but because the issue of validity under international law "touches . . . the practical and ideological goals of the various members of the community of nations." If this statement means something other than that there is no agreement on international standards governing expropriations, it must mean that the doctrine applies because the issue is important politically to the foreign state. If this is what the Court means, the act of state doctrine has been expanded to unprecedented scope. No foreign act is subject to challenge where the foreign nation demonstrates that the act is in furtherance of its practical or ideological goals. What foreign acts would not be so characterized?[27]

Precisely what the majority opinion means when it says that some "questions of international law" may be handled by American courts is not made clear, and the legal world is left to ponder this dangling suggestion. It would seem fair to

[27] *Id.* at 959 n. 23.

note, however, that the Court ruling apparently relegates American courts to a position where they may use only international law rules which all nations accept, namely, truisms —not rules.

The redoubtable Mr. Dooley would probably have described the *Sabbatino* case to his friend Hinessy thus:

'Twas their foinest hour sinse th' day they decided that th' constitooshn don't follow th' flag. First th' Cuebins sthole th' American's ball an sint it to Noo York. Th' Americans begin t' argy with thim befure th' supreme coort abhout who ownded th' thing. Thin Kennedy's man Katzenjammer cum up prothestin he don't care who owns th' ball but th' State Dephartmint was goin t' quartherback th' taim. At that me bruther Whizzer White takes humbridge n' cumminsiz a thund'rus dissint. He don't know 'r care who owns th' ball 'r who quartherbacks s'long as th' game is played undher innernashunal rools. Sum curiyus Americans standin' on th' sidelines enther th' argymint, sum iv thim in favor iv local rools n' sum f'r innernashunal rools—but nun iv thim concerned who quartherbacks. Afther siviral quarthers iv this me bruther Harlan throws up his hands at th' whole mess. Writin' f'r th' larned coort he obsarves there ain't anny rools in th' bill iv rights f'r th' game iv innernashunal thievery. There's not anny need f'r a quartherback, he opines, f'r there ain't but wun play t' run anny how n' thats thrue th' cinter iv the line be th' State Dephartmint. Thin eight iv thim cap it off be decidin that nun iv thim will play, sinse the larned joodishry is too stoopid t' larn anny rools. Histin their joodishial robes aroundst thim they giv th' ball to the Cuebins n' tuk thimsilfs off t' decide easier questhions.

5

MR. DOOLEY: Di-plomacy has become a philanthropic pur-soot like shopkeepin', but politics, me lords, is still th' same ol' spoort iv highway robb'ry.

SABBATINO AFTERMATH

*T*HE FLOWERING of the Act of State Doctrine has doubtless resulted from the tendency of British and American judges to accept the word-formula uncritically and thus multiply the judicial opinions in which it appears as an apparent factor. A recent commentator notes witheringly:

> In none of the principal American decisions did any question of the validity of the act of state ever arise, and therefore remarks addressed to the subject were merely obiter; but, seized upon and reiterated by judges in countless subsequent cases, the principle is now, it must be admitted, taken by many to be a separate rule which goes further toward clothing and sanctifying the foreign act of state than the normal conflicts rule would allow.[1]

[1] Zander, "The Act of State Doctrine," 53 Am. J. Int'l L. 826 (1959).

The Anglo-American principle of *stare decisis* unfortunately tends to degenerate into a principle of *stare expressis*. One suspects that the vitality of the Act of State Doctrine has always been increased not only by the literary appeal of its pretentious word-formula but also by the formidable clump of cases cited as precedent for the doctrine. So many expositions of these cases have appeared in print that there is no reason for doing the whole bit again, although they—like Durrell's Justine—apparently are a wearisome turnstile through which we all must eventually pass. Several commentators have pointed out the precise factors for distinguishing the *Underhill*, *Oetjen*, *Ricaud* and *American Banana* cases as dubious precedent for situations involving international delinquencies.[2] This entire ritual is now passé, however, since the United States Supreme Court in the *Sabbatino* case expressly acknowledged that these hard-core precedent cases do not support application of the Act of State Doctrine to foreclose judicial inquiry by national courts into seizures in violation of international law.[3] To these cases must now be added l'affaire Sabbatino, consisting of the *Sabbatino* decision itself instituting a Doctrinaire Act of State Doctrine and the Hickenlooper Amendment undertaking to modify the ruling in *Sabbatino* by congressional action.

Several disconcerting practical and doctrinal aspects arise from the *Sabbatino* ruling. Viewed in the larger context of international legal patterns, *Sabbatino* and the Doctrinaire Act of State Doctrine is an aberration.[4] Similarly, the philosophical construct which presumably undergirds the reasoning of the Supreme Court projects a fallacious and

[2] Zander, *supra* note 1; Mann, "The Sacrosanctity of Foreign Acts of State," 59 L. Q. Rev. 42, 155 (1943); Mann, "International Delinquencies," 70 L. Q. Rev. 181 (1954); Kollweijn, "Nationalization Without Compensation and The Transfer of Property," 6 Neth. Int'l L. Rev. 140 (1959).

[3] Banco Nacional de Cuba v. Sabbatino, 84 Sup. Ct. 923, 941 (1964).

[4] Appendix II explores this assertion in somewhat greater detail.

simplistic view of international legal organization and the processes of international decision-making.[5] Of greater im-

[5] A positivist notion of "law" as a manifestation of the territorial character of the state is engrained in both private and public international law. Thus the positivist construct for an international system of "legislative" jurisdiction is conceived as a global checkerboard of nation-states, each with virtually unrestricted power over whatever comes into their hands. Superior to this horizontal network of municipal law there extends "vertically" an international law arising from the consent of the individual nation-states, and which for want of a central power source amounts to little more than an exhortation for the constituent states to be moral. Pushed to its doctrinaire limits this rather mechanical visualization of international law fragments the international community into autonomous "sovereigns" omnipotent within their respective satrapies, in theory restrained only by "comity" from exercising their "jurisdiction" in any manner which suits them. See Falk, "International Jurisdiction: Horizontal and Vertical Conceptions of Legal Order," 32 Temp. L. Q. 295 (1959).

This construct postulates an obsolete static model as the basis for the common jurisdiction construct of both private and public international law. The traditional positivist model is harmfully inadequate because:

> The mechanical structure of the system of private international law flowing from the misleading fundamental model of the territorial nature of law and of laws in conflict tends to prevent private international law from realizing its true function of protecting in any international situation those interests and expectations of the parties which will best promote the viability of the international society. . . . The image of the territorial state has so far departed from today's reality that it is an inappropriate model for viewing and regulating the international consequence of nationalization.

Carlson, "Nationalization: An Analytical Approach," 54 Nw.U.L. Rev. 405, 412-13 (1959).

The traditional construct is minimally accurate, of course, only insofar as it purports merely to describe the international system of direct governmental controls over specific segments of transnational events. But like Holmes' catch-phrase that "the foundation of jurisdiction is power," it is neither the whole truth nor even a very helpful truth concerning the worldwide patterns of judicial authority in the world today. In the trenchant words of Professor Nicholas DeB. Katzenbach:

> Judicial equation of jurisdiction with power to enforce a prescription within territorial limits is, then, less an endorsement of principle than an acceptance of fact. It need not be sanctified as principle and, in fact, a different result may well obtain for prescriptions unreduced to faits accomplis.

mediate importance, however, is the fact that l'affaire Sabbatino lays bare two unfortunate matters of pragmatic concern: 1) The reasoning of the United States Supreme Court in *Sabbatino* raises problems of constitutional magnitude concerning the relationship of the three branches of our government in light of Congress' subsequent legislation on the Act of State Doctrine; 2) even more immediately, it raises questions of the adequacy of our current modes of private claims settlement in the international arena. None of these matters can be fully considered in this monograph, but they are worth examining in slightly greater detail in order to sketch out the parameters of concern.

CONSTITUTIONAL PROBLEMS

Reformulation of the Act of State Doctrine by the United States Supreme Court in *Sabbatino* has laid to rest several decades of speculation concerning the proper juris-

---

Kaplan and Katzenbach, The Political Foundations of International Law (Wiley & Co. 1961), 178. Moreover, as a recommendation of what the law ought to be the positivist construct essentially advocates judicial balkanization on an international scale.

The relevance of this lies in the essential positivist approach taken by the Court in *Sabbatino* and its insistence on the basic weaknesses of the international legal order to justify the holding. One commentator has noted:

In view of what appears to be our clear interest in encouraging more general recognition of the continued vitality of customary international law as law rather than the acceptance in its place of the lowest common denominator of state practice, the recognition of the positivist approach to this aspect of international law given by the U.S. Supreme Court this year in Banco Nacional de Cuba v. Sabbatino appears, to my mind at least, particularly unfortunate.

Excerpt from address by Arthur H. Dean at the Southwestern Foundation in Dallas, Texas, July 23, 1964, published in Hearings on The Foreign Assistance Act of 1965 Before The House Committee on Foreign Affairs, 89th Cong., 1st Sess. 585 (1965). See also the address by Robert Jennings, professor of international law at Cambridge University, delivered to the Association of the Bar of the City of New York, reprinted in Hearings on The Foreign Assistance Act of 1965, *supra* at 589.

prudential basis for the doctrine. The Doctrinaire version of the rule was grounded firmly on the interstices of the United States Constitution by the following passage in the Court's opinion:

Despite the broad statement in Oetjen that "The conduct of the foreign relations of our government is committed by the Constitution to the executive and legislative . . . departments," . . . it cannot of course be thought that "every case or controversy which touches foreign relations lies beyond judicial cognizance." Baker v. Carr, 369 U.S. 186, 211, 82 Sup. Ct. 691, 707, 7 L.Ed.2d 663. The text of the Constitution does not require the act of state doctrine; it does not irrevocably remove from the judiciary the capacity to review the validity of foreign acts of state.

The act of state doctrine does, however, have "constitutional" underpinnings. It arises out of the basic relationships between branches of government in a system of separation of powers. It concerns the competency of dissimilar institutions to make and implement particular kinds of decisions in the area of international relations. The doctrine as formulated in past decisions expresses the strong sense of the Judicial Branch that its engagement in the task of passing on the validity of foreign acts of state may hinder rather than further this country's pursuit of goals both for itself and for the community of nations as a whole in the international sphere.[6]

Whether this means that the Court engaged in constitutional interpretation or that the decision was dictated by fundamental constitutional law, clearly the Supreme Court was duly impressed with the serious decision it was making. The particular statement revealing this concern appears in the context of a passage in which Mr. Justice Harlan is struggling with the question whether federal or state law controls in foreign seizure cases, but that context does not significantly detract from the implications of the following statement regarding the significance of the decision being made: "However, we are constrained to make it clear that *an issue concerned with a basic choice regarding the com-*

[6] Banco Nacional de Cuba v. Sabbatino, 84 Sup. Ct. 923, 937-38 (1964).

petence and function of the Judiciary and the National Executive in ordering our relationships with other members of the international community must be treated exclusively as an aspect of federal law." (my italics)[7] Harlan draws back from expressly anointing the *Sabbatino* rule a Constitutional Decision, and instead characterizes the Act of State Doctrine as a "principled decision binding on federal and state courts alike but compelled by neither international law nor the constitution." Justification for the Doctrinaire Act of State Doctrine was found to reside in its "capacity to reflect the proper distribution of functions between the judicial and political branches of the Government on matters bearing upon foreign affairs."[8] This seems to state that the Act of State Doctrine in some manner derives from the United States Constitution and that it is closely related to the "political question" problem of constitutional law.

Mr. Justice White seems to have been thoroughly convinced that the majority was relying on the Constitution when it "urged that the act of state doctrine is a necessary corollary of the executive's authority to direct the foreign relations of the United States" and, moreover, that "due regard for the executive function" compels the Judiciary to implement the Doctrine. Attempting to meet the argument of the majority, he evidences his understanding of the doctrinal holding in the case:

> Without doubt political matters in the realm of foreign affairs are within the exclusive domain of the executive branch, ... But this is far from saying that the Constitution vests in the executive exclusive absolute control of foreign affairs or that the validity of a foreign act of state is necessarily a political question ... And it cannot be contended that the Constitution allocates this area to the exclusive jurisdiction of the executive, for the judicial power is expressly extended by that document to controversies between aliens, citizens or states, aliens and aliens, and foreign states and American citizens or states.[9]

[7] *Id.* at 939.
[8] *Id.* at 940.
[9] *Id.* at 957.

He would have adopted the proposition advocated by the Association of the Bar of the City of New York which explicitly recognizes both the Constitutional competence and propriety of judicial review of foreign seizures in violation of international law, unless there is an objection from the Executive branch grounded on its "primary responsibility" to conduct national foreign affairs.

A lively pedagogical controversy has arisen during the past few years over whether the "judicial restraint" doctrine of the United States Supreme Court in cases presenting "political questions" is truly Constitutional doctrine. The self-imposed rules of judicial restraint are grounded ultimately on the wording of the Constitution which allocates the judicial power of the nation to the Supreme Court concerning "all Cases . . . [and] Controversies," and the most popular interpretation of the proper scope of the Court's power seeks to formulate rules which will unfailingly screen out all non-cases or non-controversies. Thus, for example, the dispute must be "ripe" for judicial decision on constitutional grounds, the parties must have "standing to sue," the dispute must present an "actual" controversy and not a staged one, and the matter for determination must be "justiciable" as distinguished from "political" in nature. Whether these rules are truly constitutional law or merely represent quasi-jurisdictional requirements which in practice must be satisfied in order to get a ruling from the Court in a particular case remains an intriguing intellectual puzzle. Fortunately, speculation into the precise jurisprudential core of these "passive virtues" has recently been the pastime of law professors who have contributed something to the sum total of human knowledge.[10] But these professorial speculations offer little insight on the residual issue raised by the *Sabbatino* case: is Judicial nonreview of the validity of foreign seizures a matter of constitutional law?

Assuming that the *Sabbatino* decision is grounded to some extent on the Constitution, either because it represents

[10] Bickel, "The Passive Virtues," 75 Harv. L. Rev. 40 (1963).

a particular application of the "political question" rule which may be of Constitutional origin or because the majority invoked the tripartite structure of our federal government (set up in the Constitution) for a particular ruling based on the "separation of powers" theme, then fascinating questions of Constitutional magnitude should arise if the Executive tries to exercise its Bernstein exception or when Congress undertakes to legislate on the subject. It is just a matter of time until the former case arises, and the latter event has already occurred. The Hickenlooper Amendment to the Foreign Assistance Act of 1964 purports to change the *Sabbatino* rule.

Legislature versus Judiciary—the Hickenlooper Amendment

Congress appropriated $325 billion for foreign aid in 1965 and made a number of changes in our foreign assistance program by means of the Foreign Assistance Act of 1964. But buried in the middle of the bill and apparently unnoticed by practically anyone except the parties interested in *Sabbatino* was the Hickenlooper Amendment adding a new provision to the Foreign Assistance Act of 1961. Section 301(e) of the Act empowers the President of the United States to suspend assistance to any country which "has nationalized or expropriated or seized" property owned by United States citizens, "has taken steps to repudiate or nullify existing contracts or agreements with any United States citizen," or which has imposed "discriminatory taxes" or other exactions having the effect of seizing their property:

and such country . . . fails within a reasonable time . . . to take appropriate steps, which may include arbitration, to discharge its obligations under international law toward such citizen . . . including speedy compensation for such property in convertible foreign exchange, equivalent to the full value thereof, as required by international law. . . .

The Hickenlooper Amendment of the 1964 Act adds to that section a new subsection overturning the *Sabbatino* case.

106

There can be no mistake about the intent of the amendment which was added to the bill only a few months after the Supreme Court decision. The federal statute now provides:

Notwithstanding any other provision of law, no court in the United States shall decline on the ground of the federal act of state doctrine to make a determination of the merits giving effect to the principles of international law in a case in which claim of title or other right to property is asserted by any party including a foreign state (or a party claiming through such state) based upon (or traced through) a confiscation or other taking after January 1, 1959, by an act of that state in violation of the principles of international law, including the principles of compensation and the other standards set out in this subsection: Provided, That this subparagraph shall not be applicable . . . in any case with respect to which the President determines that application of the act of state doctrine is required in that particular case by the foreign policy interests of the United States and a suggestion to this effect is filed on his behalf in that case with the court.[11]

The Hickenlooper Amendment originated in the Senate bill providing for the Foreign Assistance Act of 1964 and was considerably more clear-cut than the final version enacted into law. The managers of the House foreign aid appropriation bill, which contained no Hickenlooper Amendment, insisted on three provisos in the committee of conference. The first original proviso excluded from the scope of the statute certain letter of credit situations and limited the statute to cases of foreign seizures in violation of international law. This seems to have been inserted at the behest of some finance and insurance concerns in an excess of caution who had not yet assessed the impact of the Hickenlooper Amendment on their letter of credit transactions overseas. The second proviso is quoted above, having survived alteration in 1965, and embodies the version of Act of State urged by Mr. Justice White in dissent and by the Association of the Bar of the City of New York that the Act of State Doctrine is inapplicable to cases involving inter-

[11] 22 U.S.C.A. 2370(e) (2).

national delinquencies *unless* the State Department specifically objects to judicial inquiry in the particular case on grounds of foreign policy. A third proviso in the original legislation provided that the act would have an effective life of only two years in order that a fuller study of the matter could be undertaken and the need for a permanent Hickenlooper Amendment assessed and thus assured that *Sabbatino* would be refought within two years. The Hickenlooper Amendment became a combination of the versions urged in argument before the Court in *Sabbatino* by the Executive Committee of the American Branch of the International Law Association, the Association of the Bar of the City of New York, and the defendants Farr, Whitlock and Mr. Sabbatino. This startling reversal of *Sabbatino* reveals the concern and expertise which can be mustered when businessmen and international lawyers unite on a matter of common concern.

The campaign to enact the Hickenlooper Amendment began with the formation of the Rule of Law Committee shortly after the *Sabbatino* decision was rendered. This rather pretentiously named group consisted of several prominent individuals and businesses, including the following American firms which have international business dealings:

Aluminum Company of America
American & Foreign Power Co., Inc.
American Metal Climax, Inc.
Anaconda Company
Bethlehem Steel
Chase Manhattan Bank
Ford Motor Company
Gulf Oil Corporation

International Telephone & Telegraph Corp.
Kennecott Copper Corp.
North American Sugar Industries
Republic Steel
Socony Mobil Oil Co., Inc.
Standard Oil Co. of Calif.
Standard Oil Co. (New Jersey)
Texaco, Inc.
United Fruit Co.
United States Steel Corp.

Pan American Insurance Company later joined the group, but the National City Bank of New York City stood in opposition to the amendment to the bitter end. The Rule of

Law Committee finished drafting the Hickenlooper Amendment after the House of Representatives had passed its version of the Foreign Assistance Act of 1964; so the committee persuaded Senator Bourke Hickenlooper and Senator John Sparkman to co-sponsor the legislation via the Senate Foreign Relations Committee then working on the Senate version of the 1964 foreign aid bill. It was enacted as part of the Foreign Assistance Act of 1964 without extensive public hearings.

During the next year the Rule of Law committee picked up the support of the National Association of Manufacturers, the National Foreign Trade Council, and the United States Chamber of Commerce. There was extensive lobbying by both proponents and opponents of Hickenlooper. The *Sabbatino* case itself had been remanded by the Supreme Court to the District Court for the Southern District of New York whence it had originated in 1960, and, indeed, Judge Bryan applied the Hickenlooper Amendment in the case following a hearing at which all parties—except Banco Nacional de Cuba—conceded its constitutionality.[12] Then in the spring of 1965 in the House Committee on Foreign Affairs hearings on the 1965 foreign aid bill, *Sabbatino* was replayed with embellishments.

Attorney General Katzenbach, presumably speaking not only for the Department of Justice but also for the Department of State[13] appeared in opposition to the Hickenlooper Amendment urging that to weaken the *Sabbatino* ruling would be correspondingly to weaken the negotiating arm of the Executive for no material gain. Specifically he testified that court rulings on given seizures might embarrass the

[12] Banco Nacional de Cuba v. F. Shelton Farr, William F. Prescott, Emmet Whitlock, Lawrence H. Dixon, H. Bartow Farr, Elizabeth C. Prescott, Fabio Freyre and Helen C. Downs, co-partners doing business as Farr, Whitlock & Co. and Compañía Azucarera Vertientes-Camaguey de Cuba and Lehman Brothers, 243 F.Supp. 957 (U.S.D. C.S.D.N.Y., July 30, 1965).

[13] Hearings on the Foreign Assistance Act of 1965, *supra* note 5 at 1234-71.

State Department in its negotiations for lump sum settlements. He took the position that private litigation to recover seized properties when discovered inside this country was so sporadic as to be ineffective as a deterrent to expropriations, and was positively harmful to extant recovery processes by means of government-to-government negotiation.

He was joined in opposition to the Amendment by two professors of international law. Professor Stanley Metzger of Georgetown University College of Law, who had worked as legal advisor to the State Department, echoed the statements of the Attorney General. He also added to the record his two law review articles approving the *Sabbatino* decision on that ground, and emphasized that desirable diplomatic flexibility would be sacrificed by the amendment.[14] Professor Louis Henkin, Hamilton Fish Professor of International Law and Diplomacy at Columbia University, interposed two objections. He contended that the amendment should not be attached to the foreign aid bill but instead should be considered in a separate bill by itself. Going more to the merits, he stated that the amendment was but special legislation directed against Fidel Castro and as such was ineffective.[15] Both professors conceded the constitutional power of Congress to enact the amendment but urged its impropriety because of interference with the conduct of foreign relations by the Executive as a result of court decisions on given foreign seizures in the future. They contended that the whole matter was basically a political question relating to the conduct of foreign affairs by the Executive.

The Rule of Law Committee appeared in support of the amendment through the testimony of Cecil J. Olmstead, assistant to the chairman of the board of directors for Texaco, professor of international law at New York University School of Law, and president of the American Branch of the International Law Association. Also endorsing the

14 *Id.* at 991-1032.
15 *Id.* at 1060-79.

Rule of Law Committee position were the trade groups previously mentioned and several bar association groups. Professor Olmstead made a full statement of the *Sabbatino* case and decision and also tendered for the record professional publications favoring the Hickenlooper Amendment approach and criticizing the Supreme Court decision. His oral presentation emphasized the role of private foreign investment in our national policies toward less developed nations and the disincentives to private foreign investment created by *Sabbatino*, contending these would be removed by making permanent the amendment. Pointing out that the *Sabbatino* ruling was inconsistent with our foreign aid programs, he stated that the amendment:

[I]s concerned with improving the investment climate, with all of the myriad of factors that you have in the present legislation. The Internal Revenue provides inducements for investment abroad. You have a whole range of these inducements and to have this one factor counterproductive to investment abroad seems to us inconsistent.[16]

Professor Olmstead predicted that widespread international adoption of the rule embodied in the amendment would tend to close off world markets for seized properties. He read the *Sabbatino* opinion virtually to invite congressional action on the matter, and thus had no doubts of both the constitutionality and the propriety of the legislation so far as the Supreme Court was concerned.[17]

A slightly different emphasis was given in the testimony of Professor Myres S. McDougal in support of the amendment. Professor of international law at Yale Law School, McDougal emphasized the effect of *Sabbatino* and the Hickenlooper Amendment in the context of the continuing development of international law. His letter to Senator J. W. Fulbright, chairman of the Senate Committee on Foreign Relations, states his position most concisely:

16 *Id.* at 570-620.
17 *Id.* at 613.

My greatest concern in this matter is, thus, that the United States should set a good example for other countries in the development and application of an international law designed to protect a free world society. In an interdependent world, with widely dispersed resources and skills, this must of necessity include the protection both of an international economy and of some private participation in wealth activities. Similarly, in a world without centralized legislative, executive, and judicial institutions most of the decisions about the development and application of international law must continue to be made, as during the past several hundred years, by the officials of particular nation-states. Any suggestion that our courts are not competent to continue to participate in the development and application of an international law, whether related to economic affairs or to other affairs, is fundamentally inimical to our own long-term national interests and the comparable interests which we share with other states.[18]

In the course of his testimony before the House committee, McDougal pointed out that the great bulk of international law is court-made law like our Common Law, established through a process of international claim, counterclaim, and both formal and informal decisions by national officials. He urged that the Act of State Doctrine, properly understood, calls only for judicial abstention in cases not involving seizures in violation of international law, and that "the doctrine of automatic, blanket abstention announced by the Court is clearly a new, and bizarre creation."[19] Professor McDougal took direct issue with the Court and the opposing witnesses, contending that the matter was a legal and not a political question. He set forth three points in summary: 1) all three branches of our government should participate in projecting our long-range goal of "promoting and securing a more abundant international economy and of protecting private rights; 2) our national courts should participate in the clarification and implementation of an international law appropriate to our times "as they have in the past by model

[18] Hearings on Foreign Assistance, 1965, Before The Senate Committee on Foreign Relations, 89th Cong., 1st Sess. 751-52 (1965).
[19] Hearings on the Foreign Assistance Act of 1965, *supra* note 5 at 1033-60, 1037.

behavior in applying international law"; and 3) "it is scarcely credible that the continued performance by our courts of their functions in developing and applying international law could interfere, seriously or otherwise, with the Executive's conduct of foreign relations."[20] As proof of this final point, he pointed to the proviso embodying the reverse-Bernstein power to file Executive suggestions in embarrassing cases.

The Rule of Law Committee and Professors McDougal and Olmstead fared well under questioning by the House committee members, and apparently they were persuasive. The Foreign Assistance Act of 1965 made permanent the Hickenlooper Amendment on August 24, 1965, thereby changing the rule of *Sabbatino*.

Congress' "Foreign Affairs" Power

Perhaps the Hickenlooper Amendment is not so wide as a gate nor so deep as a well, but 'tis enough, 'twill serve to challenge *Sabbatino*.[21] Yet a decision by the United States Supreme Court which rests on "constitutional underpinnings" involving "basic relationships between branches of government in a system of separation of powers" and which was pronounced with the solemnity due "a basic choice regarding the competence and function of the Judiciary and the National Executive," would not seem to be so easily swept aside by Congress.

The conduct of foreign affairs, everyone knows, is committed generally by the Constitution to the Executive

[20] *Id.* at 1039-43.
[21] S. Rep. No. 1188, 88th Cong., 2d Sess. 37 (1964). Harrowing procedural obstacles to private suits remain after the amendment. The new statute would not appear to enlarge the original owner's right to damages nor affect his right to a quasi in rem action; nor does it clarify the lurking problems of sovereign immunity to suit or service or the difficulties inherent in adapting the conceptualistic limitations of the writ of replevin to tangible property. Lowenfeld, "The Sabbatino Amendment—International Law Meets Civil Procedure," 59 Am. J. Int'l L. 899 (1965). But nobody thought the amendment ever would do these things anyway.

113

branch of our government. What may not be quite so well known is that Congress also has some foreign affairs powers set forth in the Constitution. Treaties can only be "made" by the Executive "by and with the advise and consent of the Senate," under Article II § 2 Clause 2; and, under Article I § 8 Clause 10, Congress is empowered to "define and punish piracies and felonies committed on the high seas, and offences against the law of nations." In addition, most of the other enumerated powers of Congress contained in Article I § 8 coincidentally may affect matters of international concern. Thus the basic constitutional principle of separation of powers can fairly be said to extend to the conduct of foreign affairs. However, as one commentator has noted:

Much of the controversy which takes place over the provisions of the Constitution concerning foreign affairs derives from the efforts of the framers to apply the principle of the separation of powers in the foreign as in the domestic field. . . . The framers of the Constitution seem to have kept vaguely in mind the principle that power for action should be allocated to the executive branch, while power to determine policy should be given to the legislative branch. Unfortunately, however, the line between policy and action and between the constitutional functions of the legislative and executive branches is exceedingly hard to draw.[22]

What would seem to be reasonably clear, however, is that in terms of role-playing the Executive Branch takes the lead in the conduct of foreign affairs and formulates much of the policy in that field, while Congress' role normally is to advise and consent, but not to lead. The United States Supreme Court has manifested a judicial belief down through the years that these roles are appropriate.[23]

Congress had yet a more specific basis for enacting the

[22] Swisher, The Growth of Constitutional Power in the United States 191-92 (1963).
[23] Compare the discussion on this theme by Mr. Justice Harlan in *Sabbatino* with that of Mr. Justice Sutherland in United States v. Curtiss-Wright Export Corp., 299 U.S. 304 (1936).

Hickenlooper Amendment. Everyone who testified before the House committee agreed that Congress has the authority to overturn *Sabbatino* by virtue of its constitutional grant of power over interstate and foreign commerce.[24] Characterizing the amendment as part and parcel of our foreign assistance program, enacted by Congress, all the witnesses —both proponents and opponents—assured the committee it had such power. Indeed, in an ironic turnabout the published words of Professor Henkin on this point were inserted into the record by Professor McDougal. Thus the following passage by Professor Henkin must embody the constitutional theory on which the Hickenlooper Amendment rests:

Under the power "to regulate commerce with foreign nations, and among the several States," Congress has no less authority over foreign commerce than it has over interstate commerce . . . under the commerce power Congress can reach all interstate or foreign "intercourse"; it can reach matters precedent to or subsequent to interstate or foreign commerce; it can reach what relates to or affects as well as what is commerce; it can reach strictly local commerce and activities when necessary to make effective a regulation of interstate or foreign commerce. The power of Congress over foreign commerce would then, of itself, support legislation equivalent to a large part of the law "enacted" by treaty.[25]

These sweeping statements concerning Congress' expansive and plenary power over interstate commerce are conceded; moreover, today no vital distinction is drawn between foreign and interstate commerce insofar as the Commerce Power is concerned. However, as Professor Henkin candidly admits elsewhere in that same article, his proposition is not settled law:

Let it be said immediately that there is no precedent for so broad a proposition in decisions of the Court, and little in other

[24] Article I § 8 Clause 3.
[25] Henkin, "The Treaty Makers and the Law Makers: The Law of the Land and Foreign Relations," 107 U. Pa. L. Rev. 903, 915 (1959).

authorities. Congress has not invoked such broad powers . . . [and] the courts have not had opportunity to examine whether such powers exist and are validly invoked. An implied power, never exercised or asserted, is of course difficult to prove.[26]

Despite these misgivings in 1959, however, Professor Henkin was persuaded in 1964 that "one need hardly doubt the authority of Congress to deal with Act of State under its foreign affairs power,"[27] citing to his 1959 article. And in 1965 he was completely convinced Congress had the power when he testified before the House committee.

The precise nexus between Congress' "foreign affairs" power and the Act of State Doctrine was spelled out by District Judge Bryan in his opinion in *Sabbatino* on remand in response to the assertion by Banco Nacional de Cuba that the Hickenlooper Amendment was unconstitutional. Noting that Congress' powers in the field of commerce are plenary and limited only by the Constitution, Judge Bryan stated:

It cannot be seriously disputed that the Foreign Assistance Act is a valid exercise of congressional power under the commerce clause. American investment abroad is an important part of the Foreign Assistance program. That part of the program is dependent upon whether American investors receive fair treatment from foreign governments. . . . A major purpose of the Amendment was to afford additional protection to such investors against foreign confiscation. It was designed to "discourage foreign expropriation by making sure that the United States cannot become a 'thieves market' for the product of foreign expropriations." 110 Cong. Rec. 18944 (daily ed. Aug. 14, 1964). . . . Congress determined that the national interests in the areas of foreign investment and international trade and commerce require the elimination of the act of state doctrine except where the President determines otherwise. It so provided in the Hickenlooper Amendment. This, like the Foreign Assistance Act itself, was plainly within the powers of Congress under the commerce clause.[28]

26 *Id.* at 922.
27 Henkin, "The Foreign Affairs Power of the Federal Courts: Sabbatino," 64 Colum. L. Rev. 805, 821 (1964).
28 Banco Nacional de Cuba v. Farr, *supra* note 12 at 972.

116

Upon this rationalization he held that Congress had the necessary power and by means of the proviso had preserved the traditional Executive prerogative in the field of foreign affairs.

There are several permissible readings of the *Sabbatino* opinion concerning the precise jurisprudential basis for the ruling. Emphasizing such phrases as "constitutional underpinnings," "basic choice," and "separation of powers," the opinion appears to base the Act of State Doctrine on some aspect of the United States Constitution. In this light, Congress' admitted power to enact substantial domestic programs affecting foreign commerce may not carry with it undoubted power to override a rule enunciated by the Court concerning the conduct of judicial functions by the federal judiciary. Without quibbling over irresolvable matters of legal characterization—whether the Act of State Doctrine is "substantive" or "procedural" or whether foreign seizure cases are problems of "commerce" more than problems of "case or controversy"—it is plain that the Hickenlooper Amendment is directed at the judicial activities of the federal courts.

It is also permissible to read Mr. Justice Harlan's opinion another way and call the *Sabbatino* decision an assertion by the Court of power to create "federal common law."[29] Now the use by the Court of "constitutional underpinnings" as ground for a decision is not so much improper as it is merely confusing. The Court did not seek sanction for its decision in congressional or executive policies, programs, or pronouncements, although it clearly did what the Executive asked in the case. Instead of relying on the Constitution, precedent, international law, "inherent sovereignty," or notions of comity, each of which have been suggested as bases for the

---

This line of reasoning raises the question whether the amendment reaches seized property not subject to the mother statute—the Foreign Assistance Act—or is available to a private investor only if his property was in some manner entitled to formal protection under the basic statutes embodying our foreign aid programs.

[29] Henkin, "The Foreign Affairs Power of the Federal Courts: Sabbatino," *supra* note 27.

Act of State Doctrine, the Court expressly rejected those ideas and chose to use an obfuscatory phrase connoting reliance on the Constitution and characterizing the matter as a type of political question. Whether all this equals an assertion by the Court of power to develop a "federal common law" in general, or in the more limited field of foreign affairs, or what is more likely, that the *Sabbatino* rule was merely the residual doctrine after all the desired political requirements were met, as Professor Henkin suggests, is a fruitful conundrum to be debated by scholars.

Judge Bryan placed the Act of State Doctrine on a jurisprudential base somewhat more pedestrian than either "case or controversy" or "federal common law." He characterized the Court's *Sabbatino* ruling as a statement of "judicial policy." He noted:

By applying the act of state doctrine the courts have merely declined as a matter of judicial policy to decide such issues where a decision may affect our foreign relations. The doctrine is a self-imposed discretionary rule of "judicial abnegation," 307 F.2d at 857, under which the court as a matter of policy declines to decide the issue of the validity of a foreign act of state.[30]

The reason for this judicial policy is fear of embarrassing the political branches in conducting foreign affairs. Characterizing the Act of State Doctrine as a purely self-imposed nonconstitutional limitation in the legalistic form of a continuing presumption which was reversed by the Hickenlooper Amendment, Judge Bryan thus cleared the way to turn plaintiff's "separation of powers" argument against him:

When a determination is made by the political branches charged with the responsibility for foreign relations as to where the interests of the United States lie, it is not for the courts to say them nay. The basic reason for the application of the act of state doctrine disappears. To require that the doctrine be applied despite the express directions of the political branches on the subject would be to place the court in the position of having the last word in matters affecting foreign affairs, the

[30] Banco Nacional de Cuba v. Farr, *supra* note 12 at 974-75.

determination of which is committed to other branches of the Government. This would be wholly inconsistent with the doctrine of separation of powers and with the very rationale of the act of state doctrine.[31]

Elsewhere in his opinion he reveals how the "political branches" reached a consensus on the Act of State Doctrine matter, e.g. because the President did not veto the Hickenlooper Amendment.

Congress' Power over Federal Courts

Congress has yet another string to its constitutional bow: its Article I and Article III powers to "constitute," "ordain and establish" inferior federal courts and the power to impose "exceptions" and "regulations" on the appellate jurisdiction of the Supreme Court. In the final analysis the Hickenlooper Amendment must be reconciled with the independent judiciary set up by the Constitution. Whatever else may be read out of the *Sabbatino* opinion, the following statement would seem to be the essence of the decision:

[T]he Judicial Branch will not examine the validity of a taking of property within its own territory by a foreign sovereign government, extant and recognized by this country at the time of suit, in the absence of a treaty or other unambiguous agreement regarding controlling legal principles, even if the complaint alleges that the taking violates customary international law.[32]

Yet Congress has commanded that "no court in the United States shall decline on the ground of the federal act of state doctrine to make a determination of the merits" in foreign seizure cases. Whatever the precise jurisprudential basis of the Act of State Doctrine, it is clear the Hickenlooper Amendment commands the Judicial Branch to do what *Sabbatino* says it will not do.

The first time Congress attempted to expand the duties of the Court against its will was in the Judiciary Act of 1789

[31] *Id.* at 975.
[32] Banco Nacional de Cuba v. Sabbatino, 84 Sup. Ct. 923, 940 (1964).

119

which culminated in *Marbury v. Madison* in 1803.[33] In that fountainhead case Chief Justice Marshall held the legislation unconstitutional on grounds that it purported to enlarge the original jurisdiction of the Supreme Court in contravention of the Constitution. Counsel for Marbury contended that notwithstanding its apparent unconstitutionality the act was nevertheless binding on the Court. This contention was soundly rejected because 1) "it is emphatically the province and duty of the judicial department to say what the law is," 2) the Court must decide whether the act or the Constitution controls when they conflict, and thus 3) the principle urged by Marbury would "subvert the very foundation of all written constitutions."[34] The principles of judicial supremacy over the other branches concerning constitutional interpretation, established in the case of the "midnight judges," have persevered. On few occasions since then has Congress successfully tampered with the Court's jurisdictional activities.

One case was the post-Civil War case *Ex Parte Mc-Cardle*[35] in which Congress *withdrew* from the Court appellate jurisdiction over a habeas corpus action. Two years after that case was decided its effect was stringently limited by another decision[36] and, more recently, Justices Douglas and Black noted "there is a serious question whether the McCardle case could command a majority view today."[37]

On several occasions, however, Congress has effectively exercised its constitutional powers under Article III to create "judicial" federal courts or legislated so as to affect the jurisdictional activities of these inferior courts.[38] Not

[33] 1 Cranch 137 (1803).

[34] *Id.* at 178.

[35] 7 Wall. 506 (1868).

[36] Ex Parte Yeager, 75 U.S. (8 Wall.) 85 (1869) (Act limited to McCardle case).

[37] Glidden Co. v. Zdanok, 370 U.S. 530, 605 n. 11 (1962).

[38] See Hart, "The Power of Congress to Limit the Jurisdiction of Federal Courts: An Exercise in Dialectic," 66 Harv. L. Rev. 1362 (1953).

only has it created "legislative" courts of various types under its Article I powers—such as the Tax Court and Court of Claims—but Congress has also conferred Article I powers on Article III federal courts. Yet when the validity of an exercise of this latter exertion of Congressional authority was litigated before the Supreme Court in 1949 the reasoning of individual members of the Vinson Court went off in every possible direction, and it is not clear what the Warren Court would do with another *Tidewater Transfer* case.[39]

[39] National Mutual Insurance Co. v. Tidewater Transfer Co., 337 U.S. 582 (1949). The majority opinion in this case, written by Mr. Justice Jackson, contains two points of importance in this context. It was contended in argument before the Court that Congress could not confer on Article III courts jurisdiction over suits brought by citizens of the District of Columbia because:

> no jurisdiction other than specified in Art. III can be imposed on courts that exercise the judicial power of the United States thereunder . . . [and] Article I powers over the District of Columbia must be exercised solely within that geographic area. *Id.* at 590.

He responded to the first point by referring to the separation of powers theme of "our system" which was not necessarily grounded on Article III or any other particular provision of the Constitution "but because 'behind the words of the constitutional provisions are postulates which limit and control,' " and thus there were limits to the duties Congress may impose on federal courts. His primary point was that Congress had wide latitude in the selection of means to implement its policies under its Article I powers, and that Article III courts, although limited to exercise of "judicial power," could receive that power from both Article III and Article I. He then noted:

> Many powers of Congress other than its power to govern Columbia require for their intelligent and discriminating exercise determination of controversies of a justiciable character. In no instance has this Court yet held that jurisdiction of such cases could not be placed in the regular federal courts that Congress has been authorized to ordain and establish. *Id.* at 592.

Mr. Justice Rutledge did not believe this could be done, *id.* at 607, although he concurred in the result reached by the majority. The final lineup was Jackson, Black and Burton concurring in the majority opinion with Rutledge and Murphy concurring in the result but not the reasoning. Chief Justice Vinson agreed with Rutledge on the point here being noted, but filed a dissenting opinion, as did Mr. Justice Frankfurter, with whom Mr. Justice Reed concurred, asserting that Article III defined the limit of the jurisdictional capacity of constitu-

121

District Judge Bryan in the remanded *Sabbatino* case touched all these bases in his opinion, and further noted several examples wherein formally announced judicial rulings of abstention were changed by "Congress directing that issues on which the courts had abstained should be decided."[40] He seemed to be relying on the *Haworth*[41] and *Yakus*[42] cases when he held:

It seems clear that when Congress, dealing with subject matter within the powers delegated to it by the Constitution, speaks with respect to a voluntary judicial policy of self-limitation, the courts are bound to follow its directions unless compelled not to do so by the Constitution. There is no constitutional compulsion to disregard the directions of Congress as to the elimination of the self-imposed limitation of the act of state doctrine as provided in the Amendment.[43]

The crux of the matter insofar as Judge Bryan is concerned is that Congress has spoken and that's that.

When all was said and done Judge Bryan held that the Hickenlooper Amendment applied so as to bar application of the Act of State Doctrine in the particular case. But he took cognizance of the reverse-Bernstein Exception in the Hickenlooper Amendment and delayed giving a final judgment in favor of the defendant for sixty days in order to afford the Department of State an opportunity to exercise

---

tional courts which could not exercise powers conferred by Congress under Article I.

The most recent case considering this matter of congressional power under Articles I and III is Glidden v. Zdanok, 370 U.S. 530 (1962), which held that Congress could convert Article I courts into Article III courts by bare legislative statement to that effect. The majority opinion was written by Mr. Justice Harlan implying, charged Mr. Justice Douglas, "that Congress could vest the lower federal courts with the power to render advisory opinions . . . [and] how Congress could transform regular Article III courts into Article I courts is a mystery." *Id.* at 605 n. 11.

[40] Banco Nacional de Cuba v. Farr, *supra* note 12 at 975.

[41] Aetna Life Insurance Company v. Haworth, 300 U.S. 229 (1937).

[42] Yakus v. United States, 321 U.S. 414 (1944).

[43] Banco Nacional de Cuba v. Farr, *supra* note 12 at 976.

its option and determine that "application of the act of state doctrine is required . . . by the foreign policy interests of the United States" and file a "suggestion to this effect" with the Court. One day before this sixty-day period lapsed on September 30, 1965, the Court was informed by letter from the Executive that "no such determination is contemplated." The Act of State Doctrine thus out of the case, the Court finally got back to the merits, e.g. whether the seizure was valid under international law so as to vest title to the sugar in the Cuban government and thereby entitle it to recover the proceeds from the sale.

The *Sabbatino* case ended in final judgment for the defendant on November 15, 1965, based on the previous ruling by the Circuit Court of Appeals that the seizure under Public Law 851 was in violation of international law, specifically, that the Cuban expropriation decree "failed to provide adequate compensation . . . involved a retaliatory purpose and a discrimination against United States nationals."[44]

The United States Supreme Court in *Sabbatino* rendered a most unfortunate decision, and Congress did yeoman service attempting to set things right by enacting the Hickenlooper Amendment. Judge Bryan clearly came to the correct decision in the case on remand, and did so in a thoughtful, authoritative and persuasive opinion. Yet the heart of the matter remains undisturbed. Perhaps a more fruitful line of inquiry is opened up by phrasing the issue thus: The composition of the Supreme Court being substantially the same as it was in 1964 and assuming that Mr. Justice Harlan's opinion still fairly represents the thinking of a majority of the justices on the Court, will the Court stick by its Doctrinaire Act of State rule announced in

[44] Banco Nacional de Cuba v. F. Shelton Farr, William F. Prescott, Emmet Whitlock, Lawrence H. Dixon, H. Bartow Farr, Elizabeth C. Prescott, Fabio Freyre and Helen C. Downs, co-partners doing business as Farr, Whitlock & Co. and Compañía Azucarera Vertientes-Camaguey de Cuba and Lehman Brothers, 60 Civ. 3929 (U.S.D.C.S.D.N.Y. November 15, 1965).

Sabbatino, acquiesce in the Hickenlooper Amendment, avoid the question altogether, or—perhaps—split the baby?

The significance of these speculations into the Court's future maneuverings lies in the distinct possibility that if the *Sabbatino* ruling is truly based on "constitutional underpinnings" then the Hickenlooper Amendment may be tantamount to another attempt by Congress to alter the constitutional allocation of judicial duties, which under *Marbury v. Madison* cannot constitutionally be done. The wording of the Amendment is clearly open enough, however, to make it applicable to the lower federal courts, and therefore binding on them as an exercise of Congress' Article III powers, although not binding on the Supreme Court. Congress might well be unable to force the Court to give up one of its "passive virtues," reclassify a "political question" as a legal question, or to redefine what constitutes a "Case or Controversy" within the meaning of the Constitution. But the Amendment may yet be interpreted so as to permit federal courts to play the role of legislative courts engaged in the process of administering Congress' foreign aid program. Perhaps this is how we get out of the jurisprudential box *Sabbatino* put us in.

MODES OF INTERNATIONAL CLAIMS SETTLEMENTS

The well-known diversity of international legal opinion concerning the role of private ownership of property offered another basis for the *Sabbatino* decision. Legitimate doctrinal differences between capitalist and socialist economic philosophies, complicated by the creation at a bewildering pace of new nation-states with mixed economies, have culminated in a spectrum of international legal opinion on the subject of private property rights from which no truly universal standard has yet arisen.

These acknowledged facts provide support for the contention that municipal courts should abstain from entering the field because either the law or the courts are inadequate, the former being imprecise and the latter parochial.[45] The thrust of this argument is that economic legislation is an instance of legitimate international diversity which can only be accommodated by prohibiting municipal courts from adjudicating the subject. This policy is implemented by requiring American courts to apply a "rule" that automatic

[45] Perhaps the highest refinement of this position appears in a commentary criticizing the Sabbatino decisions rendered by the lower federal courts:

> Briefly the position is this: in general, municipal courts should avoid interference in the domestic affairs of other states when the subject matter of disputes illustrates a legitimate diversity of values on the part of two national societies. In contrast, if the diversity can be said to be illegitimate, as when it exhibits an abuse of universal human rights, then domestic courts fulfill their role by refusing to further the policy of the foreign legal system. In instances of legitimate diversity, where a genuine universal sentiment exists, then domestic courts properly act as agents of international order only if they give maximum effect to such diversity.

Falk, "Toward a Theory of the Participation of Domestic Courts in the International Legal Order: A Critique of Banco Nacional de Cuba v. Sabbatino," 16 Rutgers L. Rev. 1, 8 (1961).

His point is that municipal courts participate in the international legal order by not participating: they impose on themselves the Act of State Doctrine. The justification for this?

> In order to guard against provincialism, it is best to deprive domestic courts of competence over such a case by the use of quasi-jurisdictional doctrines like act of state . . . domestic courts are not equipped emotionally or technically to cope with this confusion, and tend to invoke norms that correspond with the national preference. *Id.* at 9.

Professor Falk has since expanded his article into a book: Falk, The Role of Domestic Courts in the International Legal Order (1964).

Mr. Justice Harlan in his *Sabbatino* opinion was not quite so explicit but was no less impressed with this point. Responding to the contention that American courts could contribute to international law by inquiring into the validity of foreign seizures, he noted that the contention:

> [R]ests upon the sanguine presupposition that the decisions of the courts of the world's major capital exporting country and principal exponent of the free enterprise system would be accepted as disinterested expressions of sound legal principle by those adhering to widely different ideologies.

Banco Nacional de Cuba v. Sabbatino, 84 Sup. Ct. 923, 943-44 (1964).

125

deference be accorded foreign acts of state regarding economic matters.

Clarity is not one of the virtues of the majority opinion concerning this particular matter. The Court certainly ruled out judicial inquiry into foreign seizures in the absence of a treaty. But it is not altogether clear what else is ruled out. Mr. Justice Harlan first states that the nations of the world are seriously divided in opinion on the question of "the limitations on a State's power to expropriate the property of aliens." A footnote—doubtless intended to clarify this point —then seems to say this is not the reason for the ruling: "We do not, of course, mean to say that there is no international standard in this area; we conclude only that the matter is not meet for adjudication by domestic tribunals."[46] Even more broadly, the Court indicates that the differences in political ideology among blocs of nations which lie behind these differing national attitudes toward expropriation may well produce a great number of other types of transactions "not meet for adjudication" despite the presence of a working consensus on standards. But then promptly the matter is confused again: "There are, of course, areas of international law in which consensus as to standards is greater and which do not represent a battleground for conflicting ideologies. This decision in no way intimates that the courts of this country are broadly foreclosed from considering questions of international law."[47] The Act of State Doctrine now may be taken to foreclose judicial inquiry by American courts into the validity of a foreign seizure under *any* criteria—*unless* there is "a treaty or other unambiguous agreement regarding controlling legal principles" and then only if the matter *is* "meet for adjudication" by reason of a "degree of codification or consensus concerning a particular area of international law" so that the court has merely to "focus on the application of an agreed principle to cir-

[46] Banco Nacional de Cuba v. Sabbatino, 84 Sup. Ct. 923, 940 n. 26 (1964).
[47] *Id.* at 941 n. 34.

126

cumstances of fact" and eschew the job of "establishing a principle not inconsistent with the national interest or with international justice."

One defender of the *Sabbatino* decision, whose theoretical analysis seems to have been adopted to some degree by Mr. Justice Harlan, appears to restate the *Sabbatino* rule when he "advocates" in 1964 "judicial independence" for the Executive branch in "situational" Act of State cases. Professor Falk in his post-*Sabbatino* articles contends for a Doctrinaire Act of State rule qualified only by the single exception that where there is an overwhelming international consensus the Court can inquire into the merits of the seizure under international law. This sole exception is adequate, he says, because

> There are no developed central legal organs able to change old law conflicts with new patterns of values . . . [The] dispersion of governmental institutions on the national level and the patterns of effective control both affirm the territorial nature of law. In the absence of an overwhelming consensus to the contrary, domestic courts should accept the validity of the territorial acts of the foreign government . . . a restrictive view of judicial function acknowledges the weakness of substantive international law in a world divided along ideological, cultural and economic lines.[48]

One has the distinct impression Mr. Justice Harlan said just that in his *Sabbatino* opinion. Whatever this means, the rule now seems to be that the likeliest type of international seizure case to be decided by the United States Supreme Court under *Sabbatino* will be only those involving treaties.

The most questionable aspect of this whole approach is that it magnifies the existing diversity of international opinion concerning economic legislation and makes it an obstacle impossible to cross. There is substantial agreement in the making concerning the basic international norm: a taking must be compensated. The Harvard Convention on

[48] Falk, "The Role of Domestic Courts in the International Legal Order," 39 Ind. L. Jour. 429, 443-44 (1964).

The International Responsibility of States for Injuries to Aliens (Draft No. 12) predicates a "wrongful" taking upon the failure to pay compensation, explaining:

In light of the general recognition in municipal legal system of a government's power of compulsory acquisition of property, international law similarly recognizes the power of a State to take the property of an alien—but subject to several important limitations. The first of these is an obligation to pay compensation for the property taken, subject to certain exceptions analogous to those of municipal law . . . the taking of title to or the use of property of a alien becomes wrongful only if the necessary compensation is not paid.

International diplomatic practice has for many centuries concentrated on the process of international agreement for the necessary assurances and substantive criteria to regulate global economic and political processes. This practice has recently taken the form of negotiations for multilateral or bilateral treaties and international contracts in the form of concession agreements, instruments of approval, or investment contracts. In addition, during the past few years certain investor states have enacted municipal laws designed to encourage participation in the international economic process, while certain capital-importing states have enacted public laws prohibiting expropriations.

These are laudable ventures toward peaceful and lawful settlements of difficult international economic questions. However, it must be admitted that there are crippling limitations attendant upon each of the above legal devices.[49] A diagram showing the primary international agreement sources for policy-criteria in a typical act of state situation together with the principal defects for each source would look something like this:

[49] Friedmann and Pugh, Legal Aspects of Foreign Investment, 722-33 (1959).

SOURCE	DRAWBACKS
BILATERAL TREATIES— "Friendship, Navigation & Commerce Treaties"	U.S. has FCN treaties with only about 32 nations and they have nonstandardized terms in very general language—sole remedy is government-to-government arbitration.[50]
PRIVATE CONTRACTS— "Concession Agreements" "Instruments of Approval" "Investment Guarantee Contracts"	Disputed whether they are "instruments of international law" —violations must amount to a "denial of justice"—probably no international arbitration available.
MUNICIPAL LAW *Capital-Importing States*— "Public laws prohibiting expropriation"	No absolute assurances against expropriation given—statutes can be repealed or amended freely under international law.
Capital-Exporting States— "Investment Guaranty Insurance Programs"	Expensive and the project must be approved by government agency—coverage only for new investment—host states must sign treaty with capital-exporting state which has compulsory arbitration provision.[51]

[50] Jennings, "The Sabbatino Controversy," 20 The Record of the Association of the Bar of New York City 81, 89 (Feb. 1965).

[51] The discussion by Friedmann and Pugh, *supra* note 49, concludes pessimistically:

> Moreover, we should note that no guarantee can today provide complete security (even from non-business risks). The lack of security of investment in foreign, and especially underdeveloped, countries is due to, and is a manifestation of, the general lack of stability in today's economic as well as political situation. It is not possible to provide complete security for investment where the underlying economic and political conditions are unstable. Legal means are useful in the effort toward equilibrium but they cannot be the only means employed. . . . It is not possible to state that any of the guarantees here discussed are certain to survive a radical change in the guaranteeing country's general political, economic, and social structure. Survival is by no means sure. *Id.* at 732-33.

On the other hand, a slightly more hopeful note is sounded by Olmstead, "Economic Development Agreements: Part II," 49 Calif. L. Rev. 504 (1961), while discussing arbitration clauses in modern foreign investment agreements.

Superadded to the above-stated limitations are the well-known limitations on international judicial agencies for administering whatever substantive criteria exist. The International Court of Justice is available only when the participant states are willing to submit to its jurisdiction. Arbitral tribunals can be set up only under the same circumstances. Moreover, the harrowing procedural problems involved in litigating an international claim have been noted by commentators in tones of bitter resignation.[52]

A favored legal device for settlement of international claims which has been in existence at least two hundred years is the diplomatically generated lump sum settlement administered by a national claims commission established under municipal law. The United States and England by treaty in 1794 established mixed claims commissions which processed over 1200 claims during the 1800s. This mechanism has been established on a semipermanent basis since the end of World War II. Other familiar examples are the *ad hoc* American-Mexican Claims Commission, the American International Claims Commission (now called the Foreign Claims Settlement Commission), and the English Foreign Compensation Commission. These are often cited as effective and acceptable alternatives to judicial litigation of foreign seizure claims.

A much needed study of the American and English experience with the lump sum settlement-national claims commission device since World War II has recently been published. This study offers one of the few or perhaps the only factual exposition of the specific amounts of settlement and the administrative procedures involved. Several relevant points are made: 1) procedures are nonadversary, 2) the United States Supreme Court has held repeatedly that

[52] Young, "Remedies of Private Claimants Against Foreign States," 3 Inst. of Private Investments Abroad 45 (Southwestern Legal Foundation 1961). The Hickenlooper Amendment solved none of these preexisting problems. But no complaints on this score have been registered by private practitioners or their clients.

"a lump sum is a national fund to be distributed by Congress as it sees fit" and does not treat the sum as a trust fund held for the benefit of the private claimants, and 3) there is little or no possibility of judicial review by American courts. The study concludes that these commissions "may sometimes be thought of primarily as expedient devices for settling international claims and only secondarily as expositors of international law," and calls for a "critical evaluation" of the efficacy of the device in helping promulgate international law. A fair generalization would thus seem to be that although the lump sum settlement-national claims commission device may be a minimally (or less) adequate method for *distributing* money obtained in settlement, its admitted virtues relate almost not at all to the problem of determining national liability for seizure under certain criteria, nor does this device provide an *immediate* and effective remedy to the private claimant.[53]

The dollars-and-cents effectiveness of the lump sum settlement device leaves something to be desired, although Professor Lillich summarizes his findings thus:

To sum up, in the past dozen years or so the FCSC and its predecessors have processed a total of more than 600,000 claims, issuing nearly 400,000 awards in an amount exceeding 500 million dollars. Although these awards have not always been paid in full, in excess of one-third of a billion dollars has been awarded to American claimants.[54]

These figures may agree only roughly with those of Attorney General Katzenbach when he testified before the House Committee on Foreign Affairs concerning the Foreign Assistance Act of 1965. At that time he testified that since 1941 the FCSC had made awards to American nationals totaling $180,447,438 and that of this sum $158,037,700 had actually been paid, while claims for nationalizations by

[53] Lillich, "International Claims: A Comparative Study of American and British Postwar Practice," 39 Ind. L. Jour. 465 (1964).
[54] *Id.* at 479.

Poland in 1960 and Yugoslavia in 1964 were still pending.[55] No comprehensive account of the total dollar value of expropriated properties is available, but Professor Olmstead estimated "it would certainly be somewhere in the neighborhood, including the Cuban takings, of one and a half to two billion dollars—probably nearer two."[56] Perhaps the comments of Congressman Farbstein made during the course of the Attorney General's testimony before the House Committee on Foreign Affairs indicates the attitude of Congress toward the relationship between the lump sum settlement commission approach and the private litigation approach: "[W]hy can't we seize our own property when it is in this country and at the same time have the State Department negotiating through whatever means they deem desirable in order to secure recovery for expropriated property? Why can't the two of them be invoked? Why are they mutually exclusive?"[57]

[55] Hearings on the Foreign Assistance Act of 1965, *supra* note 5 at 1236.
[56] *Id.* at 609.
[57] *Id.* at 1245.

_6_

MR. DOOLEY: I will on'y say that hinceforth th' policy iv this gover'mint will be as befure not to bully a sthrong power or wrong a weak, but will remain thrue to th' principle iv wrongin' th' sthrong an' bullyin' th' weak.

A NEW JUDICIAL POLICY BASIS

A JUDICIAL POLICY appropriate for Act of State Doctrine situations lies within the framework of the current national and international consensus and concerns both the political and economic processes of the world community. A realistic Act of State Doctrine for American courts can and should be judicially formulated to satisfy legitimate international and national demands. The Hickenlooper Amendment offers the foundation. Frank appraisal of contemporary political, economic, and juridical factors is the point of beginning for the venture.

AMERICAN FOREIGN POLICY

American foreign policy since World War II has been dominated by the Cold War. Our temporary military alliance with the Soviets against Hitler did not last for long after the defeat of Nazi Germany. Then the American people discovered:

. . . that this earnest and upright partner was not there at all, and that in his place there was only another one of these great inexplicable monsters, more formidable this time than all the others, sitting astride the resources of half the world and the prostrate peoples of eastern Europe and China, sitting there and grinning inscrutably at us like some graven image, like something really out of this world: committed to the encompassing of our ruin, inaccessible to our words and reasoning, concerned only for our destruction. And now it suddenly occurred to many people what dangers could reside in the association of the dominant portion of the physical resources of Europe and Asia with a political power hostile to ourselves.[1]

The response of the United States under President Truman could be summed up in the phrase "military containment," and successful military actions in Greece, Iran, and Korea managed to contain the Soviets. Under President Eisenhower the phrase became "ideological containment" and the word "liberation" was used, but there was no liberation of any territory dominated by the Russians, and the hollow rhetoric of the policy was tragically demonstrated by the abortive Hungarian revolt in 1956. The Kennedy administration foreign policy was somewhat less militarily ambitious than liberation and more affirmative than mere military containment. In the words of Walt Whitman Rostow, head of the State Department policy planning board:

We seek to build a community of independent nations, their governments increasingly responsive to the consent of the governed, cooperating of their own free will in their areas of interdependence, settling their disputes by peaceful means. On the basis of this kind of community of free nations, we seek by every means at our disposal compatible with our own security and that of other free nations to bring the arms race under

[1] Kennan, Realities of American Foreign Policy (1954 Stafford Little Lecture Series at Princeton University) 26-27 (1954).

control and to move the nations now under Communist control toward acceptance of the principles of national independence, human freedom, international legal order, and peace.[2]

Translation of this policy for Africa and South America is to help build stable, peaceable, and economically sturdy nations. According to this foreign policy we must face up realistically to the hard facts of a world of rapid social change and, possibly, recurrent revolutions. Secretary of State Rusk, speaking to the Senate Committee on Appropriations for foreign aid in September 1962, made the following observations concerning the prospects for the future:

There are now 108 members in the United Nations and there will be more before this nationalist movement runs its course. That means a number of things to us. It means that it greatly complicates the conduct of our foreign relations. We can expect as we look ahead indefinitely into the future that there will be 20 or 25 changes in government every year . . . it means that we can expect a dozen minor or major crises each year simply in connection with the transfer of power . . . leaders who find themselves under the compelling demand on the part of their own people to get on with the problems of economic and social development, and who have to face the facts, find that it is easier to conduct a revolution than it is to build a nation.[3]

The Kennedy foreign policy cannot be summed up in a single word but is essentially "economic development with political responsibility" by the developing nations in the larger context of the famous political slogan for his administration—The New Frontier.

President Johnson inherited this policy upon assuming office, but his speeches during the spring of 1964 indicate he may eventually develop a foreign policy in some manner similar to that of Franklin D. Roosevelt's "Good Neighbor Policy" of the 1930s. Perhaps more indicative of things to come in the field of foreign relations, especially with respect to South America, was his appointment of Thomas C.

2 *Time*, May 3, 1963, p. 20.
3 Hearings on H.R. 13175 Before the Senate Committee on Appropriations, 87th Cong., 2d Sess. 767-68 (1963).

136

Mann, Assistant Secretary of State as special adviser on Latin American affairs, and the subsequent resignation of Theodore Moscoso, former Alliance for Progress official. Mann is popularly believed to favor a more "pragmatic" policy toward South American military coups, and as evidence of that attitude, the United States announced in the spring of 1964 that it would no longer employ the diplomatic gambit of withholding of recognition from illegal Latin American regimes as punishment. The policy was exercised with alarming speed in May 1964 when the Brazilian army overthrew the constitutional government of that country and forced President Goulart into exile. The United States recognized the military junta government within a matter of hours thereafter. *Time* on March 30, 1964, observed: ". . . there is no doubt that Latin Americans detect a new toughness in U.S. policy toward them these days—a greater insistence on U.S. self-interest and a somewhat less passionate commitment to sweeping social and economic reform than was true under President Kennedy." The clearest statement concerning our long-range foreign policy posture toward the nations of South America was made recently in the context of a speech to the United States Senate by J. William Fulbright, chairman of the Senate Foreign Relations Committee. The speech was entitled "Foreign Policy—Old Myths and New Realities," and although his suggestions concerning our short-range policies toward Cuba provoked denials from Secretary of State Rusk, it is significant that the following passage not only echoes the statements of Secretary Rusk previously quoted but also sketches out our present policy structure concerning the South American area:

The policy of the United States with respect to Latin America as a whole is predicated on the assumption that social revolution can be accomplished without violent upheaval. This is the guiding principle of the Alliance for Progress and it may in time be vindicated. . . . In Latin America, the chances for such basic change by peaceful means seem bright in Colombia and Venezuela and certain other countries; in Mexico, many basic changes have been made by peaceful means, but these came in the wake of a violent revolution. In other Latin American countries, the power of ruling oligarchies is so solidly established and their ignorance so great that there seems little prospect of accomplishing economic growth or social reform by means short of the forcible overthrow of established authorities . . . We must not, in our preference for the democratic procedures envisioned by the Charter of Punta del Este, close our minds to the possibility that democratic procedures may fail in certain counties and that where democracy does fail violent social convulsions may occur.[4]

Predictably, as in the past, Senator Fulbright will doubtless turn out to be one of the major architects of our national foreign policy. American policy toward South America has since 1930 consistently reflected a democratically flexible attitude. Senator Fulbright may have been saying that there are many political roads to modern industrial democracy, to paraphrase a communist slogan. Mexico, Venezuela, and Puerto Rico have taken different routes.

Following the Mexican Revolution of the middle 1930s that country's gross national product has tripled; 20 million acres of land have been redistributed to 2.5 million Mexican families; and national investment has increased thirty times. This was done under a political structure in which all political power was concentrated in a single political party (the Institutional Revolutionary Party), an economic structure composed of 100 percent-government-owned oil production, railroads, most iron and steel facilities, and half the nation's financial resources, and a society which is characterized by free speech and a high degree of civil liberty for its citizens.

Venezuela has taken the path of enlightened military oligarchy, and largely by virtue of gigantic American direct investments in the extractive and manufacturing sectors of the Venezuelan economy since 1950, that nation has achieved dramatic economic growth and a political stability which was able to resist violent Cuban subversive attempts to wreck its first democratic election in the spring

[4] 110 Cong. Rec., no. 56, March 25, 1964.

of 1964. Under President Betancourt, Venezuela's gross national product has been growing 4.5 percent annually; foreign debt has been reduced from $1 billion to $192 million; and 4.5 million acres of land were redistributed to peasant families. Venezuela now boasts the highest per capita income in the entire South American area.

Puerto Rico chose the path of cooperative self-help in 1942 through Operation Bootstrap by inviting American companies to locate there, offering political stability, tax advantages, and a large labor pool. Ten years later the island's gross national product has quadrupled from $287 million to $1 billion and by 1964 it was $2.2 billion; unemployment has been forced down from over 30 percent to 12.8 percent and Puerto Ricans were second only to Venezuelans in per capita income in Latin America. American investors are still putting money into this small island at the rate of $1 million a day. Fifty-two major American corporations have plants located there, and in 1964 the total number of Operation Bootstrap plants was 1,030.

These are impressive achievements but they are outstanding examples and not typical instances. Latin America's per capita income is only about one-sixth of ours; over 30 percent of the 200 million Latin Americans live completely outside a money economy and exist by barter; and one-fourth of that continent's inhabitants live on less than one-third the calories per day Americans consume. Moreover, the South American economic growth rate is so low that it is only able to stay even with the population explosion by straining every muscle. During the 1950s Latin America received about $23 billion in foreign private and public capital, but in that same period paid out $13.4 billion in capital costs (interests, profits and dividends) and lost $10.1 billion in trade deficit terms—realizing a net capital loss of $500 million. Latin American foreign exchange reserves decline about 7 percent a year, and foreign debts double every five years.

Congress and the Executive branch take these grim

facts into account when framing our South American poli-cies, but the ostrich-like attitude of the Judicial branch in the *Sabbatino* case stands in amazing contrast to that of the Legislative and Executive branches of the American govern-ment. We have made a massive, national commitment to Latin America in the form of money, moral support, and imagination during the past twenty years. Both the Execu-tive and Legislative branches have encouraged private invest-ment in that area as consistent with our policy. Conse-quently, one of the most difficult points to accept in the Court's opinion in *Sabbatino* is the rather cavalier dismissal of the contention urged by amicus curiae that the inter-national law exception to the Act of State Doctrine would encourage existing and prospective American investors con-cerning their South American investments by subjecting such seizures to judicial scrutiny. The Court belittled the idea. Yet historical facts tend to establish the proposition that foreign expropriations have finally begun to register on the private investment community in the major capital-exporting nations to the detriment of such areas as South America.

AMERICAN PATTERN OF
PRIVATE FOREIGN INVESTMENT

The partial summary of international expropriations over the past forty years which appeared at the beginning of this monograph indicates that some thirty major countries have nationalized significant portions of their national re-sources, some owned by foreigners, within the past four decades. This should have scared off the investors, but it did not begin to do so until recently.

Stock and Flow

The amazing thing about the expropriations is that during the period of time in which foreign seizures of alien-owned property have been on the upgrade private foreign investment by American investors has not only quickened commensurately but has materially outstripped the nationalization rate. The following illustration indicates this growth of private foreign investments by Americans over the period 1915-1963:

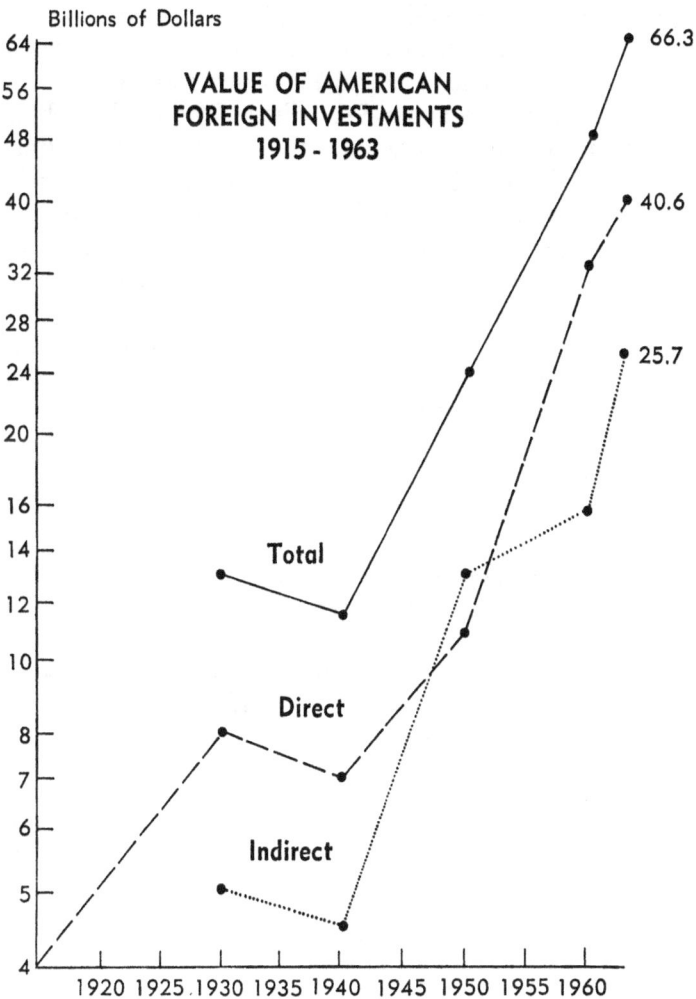

Billions of Dollars

VALUE OF AMERICAN
FOREIGN INVESTMENTS
1915 - 1963

Total

Direct

Indirect

66.3
40.6
25.7

Not only has the total value of direct investments abroad by Americans increased, but the annual flow of capital abroad has shown a similar rate of increase in recent years, even as nationalizations were occurring frequently, for example, during the 1950s and early 1960s.[5]

American investments aboard, direct and indirect, totalled about $66.3 billion at the end of 1963, even after writing off the $956 million lost in Cuba in 1960-1961. Indirect foreign investments (in the form of foreign issued securities) were valued at about $26 billion and direct investments amounted to about $41 billion. The total stock of foreign investment by Americans was increasing at that time at a rate of about $4 billion each year. This is a sizable amount of money, but the United Nations Committee on Social Affairs and Economics has indicated that a desirable, perhaps necessary, prerequisite for the economic development of the underdeveloped two-thirds of the world is the annual net outflow from creditor nations to debtor nations of 1 percent of their combined GNP. This would represent a substantial increase over the 0.86 percent average in 1959.[6]

Direction

American foreign investment has traditionally flowed outward from this country in proportions of about one-third to Canada, one-third to the South American area, and the remaining one-third scattered around the rest of the world.

Both the direction and magnitude of U.S. investments abroad during the post-World War II period up to 1960 remained in the traditional pattern, steadily growing each

[5] Report of the Secretary General, Economic Development of Underdeveloped Countries—International Flow of Long-Term Capital and Official Donations, 1959-1961, U.N. Gen. Ass. Off. Rec. 17th Session, Annexes, Agenda Item No. 35(a) at p. 49 (a/5195) (1962). The figures for the other major capital-exporting nations, including Japan, West Germany, Holland, England, and Switzerland, for the relatively stable periods immediately before and since World War II show similar increases at approximately the same rate.

[6] Report of the Secretary General, *supra* note 5.

year, increasing in magnitude but decreasing slightly in the proportion going to the Latin American area. United States direct investments in the Latin American area increased 96 percent during 1950-1958, while investment in Canada rose 149 percent, Western European investments rose 155 percent, African investments rose 175 percent, and investments in the rest of the world rose 142 percent. The following table shows the amounts involved in selected years:[7]

	1950	1957	1958	1959	1960
Canada	3,579	8,769	10,310	11,198	11,804
S. America	4,445	7,434	8,120	8,387	8,166
Africa	287	664	833	925	1,970
Asia	1,001	2,019	2,237	2,291	2,482
Other	743	2,357	3,004	3,296	3,506
Total (in millions)	10,055	21,243	24,504	26,097	27,928

The advent of the European Economic Community and the Common Market began attracting increasing amounts of U.S. foreign capital during the early 1950s, and there seems to have developed during that decade a general international pattern whereby the more developed nations began trading and investing more among themselves.[8] The significance of this recent pattern shift consists largely in its impact on the traditional recipient regions which tend to suffer unequally from a declining flow when there are redirections of the prevailing money into different areas. Thus, flows to Southeast Asia and the Middle East increased, while net receipts by Latin American countries as a group declined, and Africa became a net exporter of funds owing to capital repatriation from several countries, particularly from South Africa.[9] Another aspect of the recent shift is that within

[7] The original source was the U.S. Department of Commerce, "Survey of Current Business," August 1959. The pattern would be even more pronounced except for the whopping outflow of over $1.2 billion to Venezuela alone in 1957-1958 which tends to bolster the South American total although it likely was a one-shot maneuver likely not to be repeated soon.

[8] Report of the Secretary General, *supra* note 5 at 48.

[9] *Id.* at 53.

the various regions the uneven distribution of inflows among individual countries was magnified. Four or five developing countries now get half the total development capital while more than half of the underdeveloped countries share less than one-tenth of the total.[10]

There are a multitude of reasons for the diminished outflow and the shifting of investment flow from one territory to another, but political troubles are coming to be more important on an international scale. A United Nations committee recently observed:

In some countries, restrictions on foreign capital, which governments had imposed in the past as a protection against excessive foreign influence on the domestic economy, may still have operated as a disincentive to foreign investment. There have also been cases where political instability and uncertainties regarding capital repatriation and the transfer of earnings have tended to discourage the inflow of funds.[11]

Fears of foreign nationalizations thus appear finally to have begun exercising substantial influence over American private investors. This is almost impossible to measure by objective criteria but a recent Stanford Research Study report indicates that the first consideration to an American private investor is the possibility for profit, and then there are a series of "political" considerations including the probability of seizure by the host government. These political considerations have apparently become so important with respect to some politically unstable areas of the world that even the desire for profit fails to entice American capital. An American Bar Association Committee report estimates cautiously that "literally billions of dollars have been held back from foreign private investment because of investor's fears of non-commercial risks."[12]

[10] *Id.* at 86.
[11] *Id.* at 87.
[12] Amer. Bar Association, Committee on International Trade and Investment, Section of International and Comparative Law, "The Protection of Private Property Invested Abroad," pp. 4-5 (January 1963).

144

Redirection after Castro

The Cuban nationalizations in 1960, however, occurred in the context of a striking regional economic picture and may have been the straw that broke the camel's back for American investors. The Latin American area has been described by the nonpartisan United Nations Committee on Economic and Social Affairs as one where there is

> centred the conditional support of foreign investment influenced by the theory that profits and remittances form an uncompensated drain on exchange resources, by demands that foreign capital should complement and not compete with domestic industry, and by pressure on Governments to channel foreign investment into basic or new sectors, limit profit and dividend remittances and progressively nationalize foreign enterprise.[13]

Nationalization of the Cuban sugar company was directed primarily at American-owned assets located in Cuba in retaliation for our act of cutting the Cuban sugar quota. The following table indicates the dispersion and magnitude of U.S. private investments in Latin America in the period 1950-1960, immediately prior to the Cuban nationalizations:

This statement is further substantiated by the following: Robert Garner, then president of the International Finance Corporation, places $500 million of private capital as a conservative estimate of the funds held back from Latin American investment purely as a result of the Cuban nationalizations. . . . [A]nd one U.S. company has gone on record that, with reasonable protections against noncommercial risks, it would increase its foreign investment by some 50%—about $250 million—over a five-year period.

[13] U.N. Dep't of Economic and Social Affairs, "Foreign Private Investments in the Latin American Free-Trade Area," 14 (1961).

	1950	1957	1959	1960
Cuba	642	849	956	
Dom. Republic	106	88	104	105
Guatemala	106	106	132	131
Honduras	62	108	110	100
Mexico	415	739	758	795
Panama	58	201	327	405
Argentina	356	333	366	472
Brazil	644	835	828	953
Chile	540	666	729	738
Colombia	193	396	401	424
Peru	145	383	428	446
Uruguay	55	57	45	47
Venezuela	993	2,465	2,690	2,569
Other	131	207	248	256
Total (in millions)	4,446	7,433	8,122	7,441

A total of $8.7 billion in direct U.S. foreign investments was located in the Latin American countries by the end of 1961.[14]

Significant distortion of the traditional American foreign investment pattern began during 1961 and 1962 following the Cuban seizure of some $956 million in American direct investments in 1960. When the assets had to be written off the books of American corporations our private investors began to react. A prominent trade journal noted this trend early in 1962 and commented:

Direct investments are affected by the much reduced rate of growth of industrial production in Europe, by unsettled conditions in some countries of Latin America, economic difficulties in Canada, and more than adequate productive capabilities for raw materials at current levels of demand . . . [s]ome sizeable adjustments were made to the valuations of direct investments as of the end of 1961 which had the net effect of reducing the aggregate book value by about $0.6 billion. The largest change

[14] Pizer and Cutler, "Expansion in U.S. Investments Abroad," U.S. Dept. of Commerce, 42 Survey of Current Business 18 (1962). Total foreign investments in the South American area are estimated to have increased from $6 billion in 1946 to about $13 billion in 1958, with almost 70% of this consisting of United States capital. The bulk of U.S. capital in this area has been located in Brazil, Mexico, Venezuela and Cuba.

resulted from eliminating from these tabulations Cuban investments. . . .[15]

What started as a trend has become a major shift in international capital movement which is translated into a diminished outflow of investment by American private investors and a redirection of the existing outflow away from nations feared likely to nationalize without paying compensation.

A comprehensive survey of the entire matter of American foreign investment patterns appeared in the March 1963 issue of the U.S. Department of Commerce publication *Survey of Current Business* which noted that "Direct investments in the second half of 1962 were about $330 million, or about $125 million less than in the second half of 1961." The article discusses capital movements during 1962 in general, detailing the decline in American capital outflow and especially noting changes in the investment flow to South America:

> The recorded outflows to U.S. private capital totaled slightly over $3 billion in 1962; after taking account of usual seasonal variations, the flow declined since the second quarter of the year and registered an annual rate of $2.9 billion in the final quarter. Overall flows down by about $1 billion, purchases of foreign equity securities down by $0.3 billion, and the direct-investment flow slightly reduced.
>
> The figures also indicate a substantial shift in our balance with Latin America from net payments of about $230 million in the last quarter of 1961 to less than $30 million in the last quarter of 1962. This shift parallels an even larger one in the third quarter and thus seems to have been more than a temporary development.[16]

Permanent distortion of the traditional American pattern of private direct investment in the Latin American area has apparently now become a fact of international economic life. The August 1964 issue of the *Survey of*

[15] *Id.* at 19.

[16] Lederer, "The Balance of International Payments in the Fourth Quarter and Year of 1962," U.S. Department of Commerce, 43 Survey of Current Business 18 (March 1963) at 23-24.

Current Business notes that the long term tendency toward concentrating investments in the better developed countries continued through 1963 and into the first three quarters of 1964. The less-developed countries of the Latin American area rated the following comment: "Although the rate of investment by U.S. companies in the less-developed countries remained comparatively low in 1963, some gains were made. In the Latin American Republics the amount added to investments was $235 million, slightly less than in 1962, including capital flows of $64 million and reinvested earnings of $173 million."[17] And the accompanying tables of economic data demonstrate that the 1962 net *inflow* of $32 million from the Latin American area to the United States was supplanted by a net *outflow* to that area of $64 million in 1963. This is a far cry from the $300 million plus outflow which was annually invested in Latin America by Americans from 1950 through 1960.

A recent study of more than 160 companies with assets of about $100 million each concerning American foreign investment patterns concluded that there has been a major shift away from South America and to Asia during the recent past which promises to become more pronounced in the future. The study reported that 11.6 percent of foreign investments made by those surveyed were in Asia and some 35.8 percent in Latin America and that 46 percent of the interviewers would not recommend investments in South America. The explanation for this attitude appears in the five major determinants in order of their importance for foreign investments according to those surveyed: 1) extent of potential market, 2) political stability in the host country, 3) favorable attitude of the host government, 4) expected higher profitability, and 5) present extent of the market.[18]

The matter was put more graphically by John T. Connor, then president of Merck & Co., which operates plants in

[17] Pizer and Cutler, "Foreign Investments in 1963-64," 44 Survey of Current Business 8, 11 (1964).

[18] Louisville *Courier-Journal*, April 1, 1964, Section 2, p. 4.

Argentina, Brazil, Colombia, Mexico, Peru, and Venezuela, when he addressed a New England trade group in Boston recently: "Would you invest in an atmosphere of rising anti-Americanism, unpredictable new taxes, revolutions that occur at the rate of two or three every few months, falling profits and runaway inflation? . . . In the midst of the current chaos in Latin America, the U.S. corporation is about as much at home as a bishop in a poker game."[19] The *Sabbatino* decision discounted the importance of the international economic process and rejected a version of the Act of State Doctrine designed to implement national and international policies which aim at increased global economic development.[20]

Despite the discouraging prospect of foreign seizures of privately owned property, the United States Executive and Legislative departments have attempted to politicize the process of private foreign investment in an attempt to encourage capital flow into nations participating in such Ameri-

[19] *Time*, May 3, 1963, p. 26. Mr. Connor is now Secretary of Commerce.

[20] The United States Supreme Court dismissed the most important issues at stake as all but irrelevant when it overruled the Sabbatino solution forged by the lower federal courts because "the persuasive or coercive effect of judicial invalidation of acts of expropriation dwindles" in comparison to "the variety of means possessed by this country to make secure foreign investment"—meaning nonjudicial means. Banco Nacional de Cuba v. Sabbatino, 84 Sup. Ct. 923, 944 (1964). Professor Falk has voiced this attitude thus: "the use of domestic courts to protect American investor interests is, in any event, a sporadic, ineffective weapon, and provides little more than emotional comfort to the American investment community; more beneficial alternate means exist to improve the quality of investment protection." Falk, "Toward a Theory of the Participation of Domestic Courts in the International Legal Order: A Critique of Banco Nacional de Cuba v. Sabbatino," 16 Rutgers L. Rev. 1, 10 (1961). One can disagree categorically with every point in this statement: 1) emotional comfort is precisely what may be needed at this point in the international economic process; 2) all "legal" weapons are sporadic in this game, and the "political" weapons of the State Department have been conspicuously ineffective against Cuba so far; and 3) the existing alternate devices for investor protection are notoriously unavailable for the existing $66 billion in direct foreign investments.

can ventures as the AID and Alliance for Progress programs. The constant stream of advice from both private and public agencies continues to emphasize the role of private investment in our foreign affairs. The private investor today is exhorted to put his money into foreign investments, primarily direct investments, and particularly in South America. President Kennedy, addressing Congress on April 3, 1963, concerning the 1963 foreign aid appropriation requests, waxed long and eloquent on the role and necessity for private foreign investment as an instrument of our national foreign policy, designating national Objective No. 6: "To increase the role of private investment and other non-federal resources in assisting developing nations."[21] More vigorous action by the governmental agencies was virtually promised, and he indicated that all the branches of government should participate in "improving the climate for private investment" because "economic and social growth cannot be accomplished by governments alone."

Specifically, President Kennedy recommended two legislative measures designed to implement these policy expressions: 1) an amendment to the Internal Revenue Code to give U.S. taxpayers a tax credit for new investments in developing countries (a week later an administration spokesman indicated this would amount to 30 percent);[22] and 2) a change in the investment guaranty provisions of the Foreign Assistance Act so as to enlarge and clarify the program by broadening the coverage and increasing the appropriation for the insurance aspects of the program.[23] Attempting to

21 New York *Times*, April 3, 1963, p. 34.
22 New York *Times*, April 8, 1963, p. 1.
23 Hearings on H.R. 13175, *supra* note 3 at 20. The investment guaranty program is a step in the right direction but it has a major defect: existing foreign investments (stock) are not covered under the program and there is no feasible method of extending the insurance protection of the program to them. Discounting the other disagreeable features, such as the premium expense and the necessity for federal approval of the proposed private investment project, the fact that some $66 billion in assets located overseas are unaffected by the investment guaranty program renders it of limited

cope with our gold reserve shortage problem in the summer of 1963, President Kennedy suggested initiating a federal tax on indirect foreign investments (purchases by Americans of foreign securities issues). This produced an immediate downturn in the outflow of this kind of foreign investment. Foreclosed from our booming securities market and prejudiced by American investors' fear of Latin nationalizations, the needy countries of South America have only the possibility of increased government aid from the United States to bail them out. The pressure has become increasingly intense and in May 1964 President Johnson announced an increase in foreign aid funds would be made available to member nations of the Organization of American States.

These official sentiments in favor of economic development of South American nations are leavened by the chastening memories of nationalizations, as indicated by the celebrated Clay Committee report, published on March 20, 1963, which admonished: "Agitation for the expropriation of foreign enterprises and for nationalization of private productive ventures is hardly conducive to the mobilization of private and foreign investment and is destructive to rapid economic progress."[24]

Thus it appears that the United States government is belatedly coming to recognize its long-range dependence on international economic development in general and on the South American countries specifically. The hastily constructed Organization of American States and Alliance for Progress attest this fact. It is painfully essential to this

---

usefulness, even concerning future investments. One could cavalierly write off this tremendous investment and take the attitude that some or all of this existing stock could (and perhaps should) be immediately nationalized in the name of international economic development of underdeveloped nations. But the impact on the annual outflow from the U.S. (about $4 billion) would doubtless be disastrous.

[24] Report to the President of the United States from the Committee to Strengthen the Security of the Free World, "The Scope and Distribution of United States Military and Economic Assistance Programs," Department of State (March 20, 1963) at 13.

country that the South American continent be organized politically in some stable arrangement friendly to the United States and that economic development of that enormous resource basin proceed with vigor. The American private investor is being called upon officially to spearhead this project by exporting his money, talents, and organization to those very South American countries where the risk of nationalizations runs extremely high.

As the United States goes, so goes the world in this matter of private foreign investment. During the period 1946 through 1958 the United States' share of the net outflow of capital on an international scale amounted to two-thirds of the total. Direct investments constituted about 90 percent of the total American private long-term investment abroad, and thus a significant change in the amount or direction of American direct investment by private investors registers traumatically on the entire international pattern of investment outflow.

In the long run the annual $4 billion outflow may be even more important than the existing $66 billion stock of private foreign investment. Economic development of the international community at this point in history depends largely on the quantity and direction of the international flow of capital from investor to borrower nations. Redirection of this flow from certain underdeveloped nations to others where the probability of nationalization is believed less tends to emphasize drastically different rates of economic growth. Politically unstable areas are often not only economically underdeveloped but also their rate of growth is substantially below that of the developed nations. American investors should be encouraged to run risks of nationalization of their foreign investments in these countries if for no other reason than that distortion of economic development merely breeds trouble for the entire world for decades— perhaps centuries—to come.

CODA

*N*ATIONS OF THE world have long maintained a comprehensive legal system among themselves in order to secure the advantages of an international economy. An elaborate set of legal principles, comprising the whole of private international law and much of public international law, embodies the best intellectual efforts of mankind expended in solving the considerable problems inherent in this grand design. The keystone of this system is the arrangement which provides for allocation of jurisdictional competences concerning events occurring transnationally.

One set of these principles authorizes a state to prescribe and apply its own policies for the regulation of particular events, usually when it has effective control over the goods or persons involved.[1] Another set of principles recommends

---

[1] Allocation of judicial business among the various courts of a given state is ordinarily imposed pursuant to a deliberate pattern by means of legislative command or inherited practices. This is the distribution of primary or direct "jurisdiction" to the internal courts. Primary jurisdiction may be subdivided according to the types or sizes of cases a particular court is to handle, or, perhaps the territory the

the honoring of such unilateral determinations, abjuring other states to recognize and thereby help to make effective these initial assertions of competence, especially when the goods or persons subsequently come under their effective control in the normal course of human events.[2] Widespread utilization of both sets of principles has been regarded as indispensable to maintain even a rudimentary international economy in the form of a flow of people, goods, and services across state lines.

An underlying purpose of the entire system of these principles is to bring about a certain stability for the reasonable expectations of the people engaged in such transnational events as are in accord with the basic substantive requirements of international law. It would be a complete perversion of the system for these principles to be so manipulated as to run counter to the fundamental purpose of the entire system. Unfortunately, the Act of State Doctrine which has arisen during the past fifty years, pushed to doctrinaire limits, tends to disrupt the basic purpose of the international legal system.

The Act of State Doctrine is framed in language of majestic simplicity which deceptively masks the contradic-

---

court is to administer, all of which refer to its "jurisdiction" in common legal parlance. A clear exposition of this use of the word "jurisdiction" by American courts appeared over forty years ago. Sunderland, "The Problem of Jurisdiction," 4 Tex. L. Rev. 429 (1925-1926). But the distinction urged there and herein has been sadly ignored and the confusion continues to be compounded. This muddled use of the notion of "jurisdiction" was one of the important doctrinal differences between Beale and Lorenzen concerning the Restatement of Conflict of Laws.

[2] "Indirect" jurisdiction, a phrase coined by Nussbaum, denotes the competence accorded a foreign tribunal by the forum through recognition and/or enforcement of the foreign award. In the absence of a central power source compelling all forums to recognize and give effect to foreign judicial awards—or other foreign acts of government—the extent to which such a pattern of deference exists can be described only by such a term as "indirect" jurisdiction or competence. The time-honored word "comity" is too encrusted with legal barnacles to serve the purpose in this discussion, in addition to being ambiguous in certain important respects.

tions within. In its classic form the Doctrine states that the courts of one country will not sit in judgment over the acts of state of another country committed within its own territory. A slightly less civilized version of the same concept is the theory that strict territoriality authorizes every state in applying its own power to ignore everybody's law. The most genteel version considers the Doctrine to apply international full faith and credit. However stated, the idea that the courts of one nation *must* defer to foreign governmental acts which wreck or undermine the international economy is a weird anomaly.

The most important economic stake in the *Sabbatino* case was not the $175,000. The larger issue may turn out to have been the fate of the long-range economic development program of the international community which now consists largely of the existing $66 billion in American foreign investments and the annual outflow of some $4 billion from American investors.

Both the international community and the United States have strong policies in favor of increased stock and flow of development capital to the underdeveloped nations of the international community. The United States private investor is the mainspring of this entire global process. Predictable fears of foreign nationalizations have already begun to be translated into diminished flow of American capital overseas and redirection of the present flow to stable and economically developed nations. The rich get richer and the poor get desperate under such policies. Complete frustration of the basic long-range international policy in favor of economic development of the globe by means of increased production and distribution of goods and services is seriously threatened by these fears.

The United States Supreme Court in the *Sabbatino* case was eminently correct in holding that the Act of State Doctrine is not a rule of international law, but on the other hand, is merely a self-imposed judicial policy limitation peculiar to American municipal courts. But the Court declined to shape that policy in furtherance of the larger policies of the world community. Definitive clarification by the Court that the Doctrine does not apply at all in the case of international delinquencies would have been a salutary judicial pronouncement. Some jurisprudential progress was made, however, in a negative manner. The contention that the Act of State Doctrine is either a rule of international law or a description of international practice based on non-participation of municipal courts in the international decision-making process has been put to rest. Nor does the Doctrine rest on inflexibly explicit language of the Constitution; instead, the Court says it springs from the separation of powers theme implicit in that document. Thus to some degree there is latitude for judicial maneuver in order to accommodate the Hickenlooper Amendment without coming into direct conflict with Congress. Moreover, the insidious Bernstein Exception was put in jeopardy if not functionally killed altogether by the Hickenlooper Amendment.

The assertion has always been indefensible that, although uncompensated foreign seizures of alien-owned property are in violation of international law, municipal courts must nevertheless acquiesce in them. A dogmatic Act of State Doctrine compels municipal courts to implement these international delinquencies. No amount of sophisticated explanation, technical distinction or assertion of jurisprudentialisms about the nonparticipation of municipal courts in international law can mask this contradiction. The Hickenlooper Amendment, with all its faults, ambiguities and limitations is an acceptable, although somewhat timid, first step toward removal of this hypocrisy from American law. The point is not that American municipal courts can by their sole efforts halt the international process of nationalization of foreign private investment assets, right every wrong perpetrated on American businesses, nor that they can, will, or should impose the "capitalist ethic" on other nations. The Hickenlooper Amendment is a policy declaration by the Congress to the Judiciary that to the extent of their jurisdiction the courts should lend whatever support they can muster to the larger task of implementing international economic development through an emerging international legal order.

There is no cogent reason American municipal courts should be foreclosed from the international judicial process of clarifying the basic international community policies concerning economic activity. On the contrary, there is every reason in favor of their participation in the continuing process of international law-making. Critics of this position do not indicate where international law is to come from if not from the process of rational decision-making, and the implication is that they appear to believe it will magically emerge from the bewildering twists and turns of day-to-day diplomatic maneuvers. It is difficult to understand how an international consensus concerning anything which can be dignified by the word "law" can thereby arise. Political and economic policies and jurisprudential differences can never be fully compromised, reconciled, and joined in a creative international order without more, rather than less, formal adjudication on just such thorny problems as nationalizations of alien-owned private property.

A dogmatic Act of State Doctrine imposed on all municipal courts would not only be utterly unrealistic, but also would tend to thwart the international community in its continuing quest for international law. That doctrine imposed on the American judiciary merely insures our own insularity. The doctrine did not effectively allocate "jurisdiction" among the national courts of this interdependent world nor did it demonstrably lessen the incidence or probability of a "casus belli." Properly understood and applied so as to inhibit uncritical judicial rejection of foreign authoritative acts committed abroad concerning assets located there, the Act of State Doctrine performs its most constructive role as a form of international full faith and credit requirement subject to international law. The dogmatic version enunciated in the *Sabbatino* case did not even serve the current or long-range interests of the country which created it.

Pressing national and international policies dictated that the Doctrine should be restated pragmatically so as to conform to past realities, satisfy present demands, and be applicable to future problems. The obvious step was to except from the sweeping prohibition of the dogmatic version foreign seizures alleged to be in violation of international law and permit rational judicial inquiry to determine legality. Permitting our domestic courts access to an arena already occupied by the domestic courts of other nations can be regarded as catastrophic only by those whose concept of international law must now be reframed to incorporate what was previously an unthinkable.

The *Sabbatino* affair affords American scholars of international law the remarkable opportunity to rethink creatively their premises, rebuild their eighteenth-century conceptual models and participate more effectively in the processes of international law-making in the future. The first step should be formation of a tacit compact with the Judiciary to act as the research and development service in the forthcoming era of judicial participation in global decision-making. Failure to seize this opportunity will neither reduce the incidence of foreign seizure cases coming before our courts nor relieve our Judiciary of its obligation to decide them. Scholarly abstention will merely assure academic irrelevance forever in the field of international law.

This study ends in the same vein it began with the following doggerel recalling the faulty conceptualism which has dogged the path of the Act of State Doctrine through the trackless forest of our judicial history. Hopefully, the Hickenlooper Amendment can help bridge the hiatus between the jurisprudence of the past and tomorrow's foreshadowed events.

The millpond of International law is lost in Academe's
Glade,
Obscured by the fog of the Pedagogue's awe and
jurisprudential shade.
Each generation a Nationalist breeze, in disregard of the
rule,
Breaks through the staid professorial trees and ripples the
murky pool.

The fog starts to swirl and begins to lift from the Vale of
Diplomacy;
And arcing through an occasional rift shine beams of reality.
The breeze kicks up ripples, wavelets—then waves, to wash
the opposite shore
And erode a bank 'til it finally caves, collapsing with a slight
roar.

"I say," says the Striped Deputy Frog, "Waves on our
personal sea?"
"Is that so?" comes a croak from the nearby log, "That
sound almost deafened me."
"I'm sure we can settle it frog to frog in our traditional way."
"We will open a fruitful dialogue and give all the frogs their
say."

From the mudbanks around the stagnant slough, frog voices
rise from the mist.
Shouting his tribe's own point of view, each urges his friends
to desist.
But the waves continue, the fog dispells, the chorus becomes
a rout.
"Who's rocking our world?" the Spotted Frog yells, "He
will just have to get out."

"Why not seek out intellectual aid?" says the frog in mottled
   grey.
"Let us solicit the Scholar Brigade—what does Dean Mud
   Turtle say?"
The kindly old Dean, awakened at last, was told the facts of
   the day.
Then filming his eyes, consulted the past, and scratched
   around in the clay.

"Quite so," he said, "This has happened anon so the Oracles
   have said."
"A nefarious fish had swirled the pond; but I'm sure he is
   now dead."
"Today's tidal wave was caused by his fry, who you can
   easily quell,"
"By nonrecognition 'til he should die." Then the Dean
   snapped shut his shell.

The breeze subsided, the fog soon returned; the pond grew
   quiet once more.
The frogs were happy with what they had learned and each
   had guarded his shore.
No fish could live in the dark, gloomy slough, and nothing
   had rocked the land.
The breeze would return in a day or two and the waves
   erode the sand.

But over the brow of the nearby ridge catastrophe was
   lurking.
For the State had decided to build a bridge and the powder
   crews were working.
The concrete bridge will bring permanent shade and the
   pilings take up room;
The calm of the International Glade will vibrate with big
   trucks' VAROOM!

A BIBLIOGRAPHY OF SCHOLARLY COMMENT ON THE ACT OF STATE DOCTRINE, THE *SABBATINO* CASE, AND THE HICKENLOOPER AMENDMENT

Falk, The Role of Domestic Courts in the International Legal Order (1964)—as of spring 1966 the only book-length study of the subject

Lightner, "The Examination of Foreign Expropriation Decrees Under International Law," 49 Calif. L. Rev. 979 (1961)

Recent Decisions, "International Law—Foreign Decree May Be Examined Under International Law," 36 St. John's L. Rev. 159 (1961)

Recent Decisions, "International Law—Sovereignty—Judicial Examination of Foreign Act of State Under International Law," 60 Mich. L. Rev. 231 (1961)

Recent Developments, "Enforcement Denied to Cuban Nationalization Which Violated International Law," 14 Stan. L. Rev. 172 (1961)

Kern, "International Law—Act of State Doctrine and Recent Cuban Nationalizations," 24 Ga. B. J. 439 (1962)

Metzger, "The Act of State Doctrine and Foreign Relations," 23 U. Pitt. L. Rev. 881 (1962)

Skousen, "International Law: A Qualification of the Act of State Doctrine," 4 Ariz. L. Rev. 79 (1962)

Swansen, "International Law—Cuban Nationalization Decree

Held in Violation of International Law," 1962 Wis. L. Rev. 386 (1962)

Tessler, "The Act of State Doctrine: Banco Nacional de Cuba v. Sabbatino, 193 F. Supp. 375 (SDNY 1961)," 47 Cornell L. Q. 659 (1962)

Weisberg, "International Law and the Act of State Doctrine," 9 U.C.L.A.L. Rev. 406 (1962)

Current Decisions, "International Law—Retaliatory Measure of Nationalizing American-controlled Corporation Invalid as a Violation of International Law," 34 Rocky Mt. L. Rev. 563 (1962)

Decisions, "International Law—Review by American Courts of the Validity of Foreign Nationalization Decrees—Release of Restraint by the Executive," 8 N.Y.L.F. 148 (1962)

Recent Decisions, "International Law—Expropriation—Domestic Court Rejects Act of State Doctrine and Holds Cuban Nationalization Decree Ineffective to Pass Title," 23 U. Pitt. L. Rev. 816 (1962)

Note, "Act of State Doctrine—Its Relation to Private and Public International Law," 62 Colum. L. Rev. 1278 (1962)

Note, "Cuban Nationalization Decree Reviewed Under International Law," 37 N.Y.U.L. Rev. 155 (1962)

Note, "International Law—Act of State Doctrine—Judicial Review of National Decree by Foreign Forum," 47 Iowa L. Rev. 765 (1962)

Note, "International Law—Limitation of the 'Act of State' Doctrine—Cuban Expropriation of American-owned Property Held Violative of International Law," 20 Fordham L. Rev. 523 (1962)

Note, "International Law—Retaliatory Measure of Nationalizing American-controlled Corporation Invalid as a Violation of International Law," 34 Rocky Mt. L. Rev. 563 (1962)

Note, "Nationalization—Cuba—Suit by Nationalizing Government for Conversion of Proceeds of Nationalized Property—Act of State Doctrine," 56 Am. J. Int'l L. 1085 (1962)

Dunbar, "Act of State in the Law of War," 1963 Jurid. Rev. 246 (1963)

Lillich, "A Pyrrhic Victory at Foley Square: The Second Circuit and Sabbatino," 8 Vill. L. Rev. 155 (Winter 1962-1963)

Zander, "Validity of Acts of State Under International Law," 12 Int'l & Comp. L.Q. 668 (1963)

Recent Cases, "International Law—Sovereign Immunity—Act of State Doctrine," 32 U. Cinc. L. Rev. 112 (1963)

162

Note, "Banco Nacional de Cuba v. Sabbatino—The Immunity of Foreign Acts of State," 9 McGill L.J. 358 (1963)

Note, "International Law—Act of State Doctrine—Judicial Review of Nationalization Decree by Foreign Forum," 27 Albany L. Rev. 304 (1963)

Note, "International Law—Effect Given by the United States Courts to Expropriation Decrees of Foreign Governments when in Violation of International Law," 46 Marq. L. Rev. 391 (1963)

Note, "International Responsibility and the Act of State Doctrine," 11 Loyola L. Rev. 341 (1963)

Goldie, "The Sabbatino Case: International Law Versus the Act of State," 12 U.C.L.A.L. Rev. 107 (1964)

Grove, "International Law—Conflict Law and Sabbatino," 19 U. Miami L. Rev. 216 (1964)

Henkin, "The Foreign Affairs Power of the Federal Courts: Sabbatino," 64 Colum. L. Rev. 805 (1964)

Laughran, "International Law—Expropriation—Act of State Doctrine," 38 Tul. L. Rev. 763 (1964)

Metzger, "The Act of State Doctrine Refined: The Sabbatino Case," 1964 Sup. C. Rev. 223 (1964)

Reeves, "The Sabbatino Case: The Supreme Court of the United States Rejects a Proposed New Theory of Sovereign Relations and Restores the Act of State Doctrine," 32 Fordham L. Rev. 631 (1964)

Rossman, "Expropriation—Act of State Doctrine," 50 A.B.A.J. 675 (1964)

Snyder, "Banco Nacional de Cuba v. Sabbatino: The Supreme Court Speaks," 16 Syracuse L. Rev. 15 (1964)

Note, "International Law—Act of State Doctrine," 10 N.Y.L.F. 206 (1964)

Note, "International Law—Acts of Foreign State—Nationalization—Effect in Municipal Law," 1964 Camb. L. J. 187 (1964)

Supreme Court, "1963 Term, International Law," 78 Harv. L. Rev. 300 (1964)

Folsom, "The Sabbatino Case: Rule of Law or Rule of 'No Law'?" 51 A.B.A.J. 725 (1965)

Lowenfeld, "The Sabbatino Amendment—International Law Meets Civil Procedure," 59 Am. J. Int'l L. 899 (1965)

Mann, "The Legal Consequences of Sabbatino," 51 Va. L. Rev. 604 (1965)

Snyder, "Cinderella's Slipper & Banco Nacional de Cuba v. Sabbatino," 25 Fed. B. J. 207 (1965)

Note, "Congress Answers the Supreme Court—Is Sabbitino [*sic*] Still Law?" 10 Vill. Rev. 509 (1965)

Note, "International Law—Act of State Doctrine—Domestic Effect of Foreign Acts and Laws," 31 Brooklyn L. Rev. 417 (1965)

Note, "International Law; Congressional Abrogation of the Act of State Doctrine," 65 Colum. L. Rev. 530 (1965)

Note, "Sabbatino Doctrine—Modified in Foreign Assistance Act of 1964," 63 Mich. L. Rev. 1310 (1965)

Note, "The Act of State Doctrine After Sabbatino," 63 Mich. L. Rev. 528 (1965)

INTERNATIONAL PATTERN OF
APPLICATION OF THE ACT
OF STATE DOCTRINE

*T*HE ACT of State Doctrine was judicially created from whole cloth in a series of court decisions rendered between 1898 and 1917. From then until the present date the doctrine ostensibly has been applied in its most extreme and dogmatic form primarily by American and English courts. The English may have repudiated it in the *Anglo-Iranian Oil* case in 1953. Application of the Doctrine has been limited to cases involving foreign governmental acts directed at private parties, most frequently concerning interests in movable property. Properly speaking, then, the phrase "Act of State Doctrine" refers only to judicial deference to such foreign governmental acts.[1]

---

[1] A comprehensive study of the subject would require analysis of the seizures during wartime as well as peacetime, but the discussion herein relates to the Sabbatino situation and thus the former are omitted. It is well to note, however, the result in Anderson v. N.V. Transadine Handel Maatschappij, 289 N.Y. 9, 43 N.E.2d 502 (1942), upholding the "conservatory" confiscations by the Netherlands government in exile. Wartime politico-military policy obviously influenced the outcome there.

Taken at face value, the Act of State Doctrine would seem to invest foreign acts of state with virtual conclusivity, a stature similar to that given local acts of state, and be thus tantamount to an international full faith and credit rule. The particular word formula for the Act of State concept seems to state that all nations accord highest respect to foreign acts of state effected within the foreign territory. American courts at first seem to have considered the Doctrine a rule of international law.[2] A representative cross-section of international practice indicates there is no such international consensus concerning foreign governmental acts purporting to extinguish title to alien-owned movables during times of international peace. Such acts of state are not at all considered conclusive by national courts.

The three following examples are set forth to furnish an international cross-section view because they offer instances in which alien-owned movables were first seized in foreign territory and the property subsequently became the subject of legal action in foreign states in which the ultimate issue was whether the forum would defer to the prior application of governmental policy by the seizing state. The pattern of deference and non-deference is not traceable to application of the Act of State Doctrine by the various national courts adjudicating these controversies.

Mexican Revolution[3]

The Mexican oil industry was substantially owned by foreign oil companies when it was nationalized in 1936-1938. Some compensation was promised, to be determined and paid after ten years, but it was not generally accepted that this amounted to "prompt, adequate, and effective" compensation. The American and British oil companies largely confined their responses to exercise of local remedies inside

[2] The *Sabbatino* case expressly held that the Act of State Doctrine was not a rule of international law.

[3] For a full exposition of the background for these nationalizations see Kuhn, "The Mexican Expropriations," 17 N.Y.U.L.Q. Rev. (1939).

Mexico followed by formal protests through their respective governments. But Compañía Mexicana de Petroleo ("El Aguila"—The Mexican Eagle—a Dutch Shell group affiliate with mostly English and American stockholders) purchased nationalized oil from the Mexican government and shipped it abroad. Some expropriated companies pursued this oil into the various countries and filed lawsuits, claiming that the Mexican act of state was ineffective to extinguish their title. El Aguila itself owned oil worth $1.7 million which was seized by Mexico and subsequently sold to Eastern States Petroleum Co. in 1938. A year later in the context of a Sherman Act treble damage action between Eastern States and Asiatic Petroleum Corp., El Aguila was impleaded as a third-party defendant by Asiatic Petroleum who claimed that El Aguila was liable for any judgment rendered. El Aguila thereupon counterclaimed against Eastern States Petroleum for the nationalized oil which the latter had purchased.

These cases can be factored into their significant aspects for detailed study by means of the following chart showing the primary facts and the winning claim:

Who	What	When	Where	Whence	Why
Petroservice of Paris (Fr. corp.) v. El Aguila (Dutch Shell co.)[4]	Title to oil seized in Mexico now located in the Netherlands and attached by El Aguila	1938	Rotterdam-Hague Supreme Court	El Aguila wins	Act of State Doctrine
Propetrol Petroservice et Petrolest (Fr. corp.) v. El Aguila (Dutch Shell co.)[5]	Title to oil seized in Mexico now attached in Belgium by El Aguila	1939	Antwerp, Belgium	El Aguila wins	Extraterritoriality theory (seizure valid because effected on Mexican territory)
Banque et Société des Pétroles (Fr. corp.) v. El. Aguila (Dutch Shell co.)[6]	Title to oil seized in Mexico now located in France	1939	Le Havre and Rouen, France	Banque et Sociales des Petroles wins	Seizure violates French ordre publique
Eastern States Petroleum Co. (Amer. corp.) v. Asiatic Petroleum Corp. (Amer. co.) & El Aguila 3rd party def.[7]	Counterclaim by El Aguila for value of oil seized by Mexico and sold to plaintiff	1939	Fed. Ct. in New York	Eastern States Petroleum Co. wins	Act of State Doctrine bars inquiry into validity of Mexican seizure

[4] Petroservice of Paris v. El Aguila, W. & N.J. 1940, Nos. 19 & 20. See also Davis & Co. v. El Aguila, W. & N.J. 1939, No. 747; Mexico v. Batsafsche Petroleum Maatschappij, W. & N.J. 1939, No. 790, Ann. Dig. 1919-1942, Case No. 7.

[5] "Propetrol," "Petroservice" et "Petrolest" v. Compañía Mexicana de Petroleo et "Tankage et Transport," 1939, La Belgique Judiciaire 371.

[6] Banque et Société des Pétroles v. Compagnie mexicaine des Pétroles El Aguila, Hague Recueil 67 (1939) p. 425, no. 1, modified S. Chr. 1943, p. 77.

[7] Eastern States Petroleum Co. v. Asiatic Petroleum Corp., 28 F. Supp. 279 (U.S.D.C.S.D.N.Y., 1939).

Iran

The 100 percent British-owned Iranian oil industry, consisting of Anglo-Iranian Oil Co., Ltd., was nationalized in 1952 by executive decree and no compensation was offered. Count Zella Zonca, who had formed an Italian company to exploit Mexican oil in 1939, became interested in Iranian oil in 1952 and purchased 400,000 tons from Iran. He sold 900 tons of this oil to the charterers of the "Rose Mary" (Jaffrate was the master, a Panamanian company was the owner, a Swiss company was the charterer and the ship flew the flag of Honduras.) The oil was loaded on board at Bandur Mashur and the "Rose Mary" sailed off mysteriously, only to arrive a few days later in Aden, a British protectorate, after being ordered there by the owners. Anglo-Iranian brought action in Aden, asserting title to the oil and claiming right to possession.

The "Nissho Maru," a Japanese ship, purchased a quantity of oil from the government-owned National Iranian Oil Co., transported it to Japan, and stored the oil on shore at Kawasaki in the possession of Idemitsu Kosan Co. (YO), a Japanese company. Anglo-Iranian sued in Japan claiming title and right to possession of the oil.

Unione Petrolifera con l'Oriente, an Italian company, purchased oil from Iran and shipped it to Venice. Anglo-Iranian brought action there against the Italian company seeking to prevent transfer of the oil until another action could be concluded in Rome against the company at the place of incorporation.

When these disputes were judicially determined the following results indicate again that only Anglo-American courts utilize the Act of State Doctrine to decide foreign seizure cases:

Who	What	When	Where	Whither	Why
Anglo-Iranian (British corp.) v. Jaffrate[8]	Oil on board "Rose Mary" in port of Aden	1953	Aden	Anglo-Iranian wins	Seizure was Act of State in violation of int. law and public policy
Anglo-Iranian (Brit. corp.) v. Idemitsu Kosan (Japanese co.)[9]	Oil stored at Kawasaki, Japan	1953	Tokyo, Japan	Idemitsu Kosan wins	Seizure was no violation of int. law
Anglo-Iranian (British corp.) v. Societa Unione Petrolifera Orientale (Ital. co.)[10]	Oil located in Venice	1953	Venice	Societa Unione Petrolifera Orientale wins	Seizure was no violation of local public policy

8 Anglo-Iranian Co. v. Jaffrate (1953), 1 W.L.R. 246.

9 Anglo-Iranian Co. v. Idemitsu Kosan Co. (YO) 2, 942 of 1953.

10 Anglo-Iranian Co. v. Societa Unione Petrolifera Orientale di Roma, Il Gazzetino 67, No. 61, p. 4.

Spain

The Spanish Civil War produced concomitant seizures of alien-owned properties which were later transported to foreign states where litigation occurred directed at problems of ownership of the movables. Aside from the many ship cases, most of which involved attempted extraterritorial nationalizations, there are three examples worth mention in the context here.

The Spanish Republican Government contracted to sell five million ounces of government-owned silver to the United States government at a time when the former was in control of the area in Spain where Banco de España had the silver deposited. The silver was shipped to the United States, but before the price was paid, notice was given the United States that the Franco government was then apparently winning the civil war, was in control of most of Spain, and claimed title to the silver. Notwithstanding this notice, the United States paid the Spanish Republican ambassador by check which was promptly cashed and the proceeds pocketed. Banco de España (now under the Franco regime) later sued in the United States, asserting title to the silver and claiming the right to possession against the Federal Reserve Bank, the shipping line, and federal depository agent who had been involved in the transaction.

The Potasas Ibéricas company, which operated a potash plant in Spain, was incorporated in Spain but was owned and operated by Swiss and French nationals. During the Spanish Civil War the plant was nationalized without compensation. Thereafter a quantity of potash from Potasas Ibéricas was transported to France where the emigré board of directors—French nationals who had fled Spain during the war—claimed ownership.

Don Alfonso de Borbon y Austria, while he was king of Spain, deposited certain securities he owned privately with the Westminister Bank in London to be held to the order of its Madrid branch as his agent. The Madrid branch closed in 1923, and the Westminister Bank was instructed by him to hold the securities to the order of Banco de Vizcaya in Spain as his agent. The monarchy was overthrown and in 1931 Don Alfonso became the ex-king, whereupon the Spanish Republic seized his property and ordered the Spanish banks to deliver up his securities to the state. Both Don Alfonso and Banco de Vizcaya claimed the securities from Westminister Bank and an action was brought in England for the possession of them.

These Spanish governmental seizure cases again indicate that American courts relied upon the Act of State Doctrine to rationalize decisions while the courts of other nations invoke traditional conflict of laws concepts to reach similar results:

Who	What	When	Where	Whither	Why
Banco de Vizcaya (Span. bank) v. Don Alfonso de Borbon y Austria (Span. nat'l)[11]	Securities in English bank to order of plaintiff bank	1935	England	Don Alfonso wins	Foreign penal law not enforced in England
Banco de España (Span. bank) v. Federal Reserve Bank (Amer. bank)[12]	5 million ounces of silver seized in Spain now located in U.S.	1940	Federal Court in U.S.	Defendants (Fed. R. Bank, ship line, depository agt.) win	Act of State Doctrine and possible double liability of defendants
Volatron v. Moulin Potasas Ibéricas v. Bloch[13]	Potash seized in Spain now located in France	1938	Marseille, Aix, Montpellier, Nîmes, France	Moulin and Bloch (French directors) win	Ordre publique (Spanish seizure violative of French ordre publique)

11 Banco de Vizcaya v. Don Alfonso de Borbon y Austria, 1 K.B. 140 (1935).
12 Banco de España v. Federal Reserve Bank, 114 F.2d 438 (CCA 2, 1940).
13 Volatron v. Moulin Potasas, Ann. Dig. 1935-1937, Case No. 68, and 1938-1940, Case No. 10. See also Société Potasas Ibéricas v. Nathan Bloch, Ann. Dig. 1938-1940, Case No. 54.

To the foregoing could be added numerous other examples involving movables in the form of intangibles or choses in action. The case of the Carthusian monks is a good example. Following the French Revolution there remained a residue of animosity and suspicion of religious orders in France. Legislation of 1817 required state approval of religious congregations, and although such approval was never granted, illegal congregations were tolerated. But, in 1901 legislation registered a changed official attitude, and in 1903 France expropriated the monastery of the Carthusian monks and drove them out of the country. The monks had set up a distillery at Chartreux during the eleventh century, had become internationally famous for their liqueur "chartreux" and during the 1800s had registered their trademark in most countries and conducted business there through local agents. When France ran them out, the monks moved to Spain and set up their distillery. The French liquidator, Lecouturier, attempted to duplicate their liqueur and in 1904 began marketing his product under their name, infringing their trademark in these countries, finally assigning the trademark to one Cusenier. At one time five different liqueurs called "chartreux" were being sold internationally under the same trademark. Both Lecouturier and Cusenier claimed the foreign trademark in numerous court actions abroad, asserting situs theories and claiming the trademarks as part of the seized *fonds de commerce*. They lost in every foreign forum.[14]

[14] Argentina: Lecouturier v. Rey, Ct. of Buenos Aires, Dec. 23, 1905, Revue Darras 612 (1907).

Belgium: Rey C.S.C. Lecouturier, Trib. Comm. of Brussels, Feb. 13, 1907, 446 Revue Darras (1907); Rey C.S.C. Fouyer, Trib. Comm. of Brussels, Feb. 13, 1907, 273 Revue Darras (1907); cour d'Appel of Brussels, May 5, 1910, Revue Darras 732 (1911).

Brazil: Rey v. Lecouturier, Sup. Ct. May 10, 1907, Clunet 1171 (1907); Rey v. La Junte Commercial de Rio, Ct. App. Rio de Janeiro, May 14, 1907, Clunet 579 (1908).

England: Lecouturier v. Rey (1910), A.C. 265.

Germany: Rey v. Dr. Levy v. Lecouturier, Sup. Ct. German Empire, May 29, 1908, Revue Darras 815 (1908).

Every instance set forth herein shows that the forum either went into the merits of the lawsuit or otherwise favored its own national by dismissal of the action if he had any substantial asset at stake: 1) the Japanese company won the Iranian oil in Japan; the Italian company won it in Venice; and the British company successfully reclaimed its oil in the British protectorate of Aden before a British court; 2) the Dutch Shell affiliate won the Mexican oil in Holland and Belgium; the French company won it in France but lost in Holland; and the Mexican company won before the American courts doubtless in part because in order to render judgment against impleaded El Aguila the judgment would have first gone against an American corporation; and 3) French directors won the Spanish potash in France, while the American court protected the silver-dealing Americans in the United States, and the British court was careful not to put the British bank in jeopardy of possible double payment concerning the Spanish securities. The chartreux cases followed true to form with the French liquidator winning in France and in a French colony (French Morocco), but losing everywhere else in the world to the local liqueur distributor. Regardless what legal rationalization was used in these litigations, the forum national was protected.

The expressions advanced to support these decisions ranged from high order abstractions such as "Act of State Doctrine," "ordre publique," and "foreign penal laws" down to legal technicalities, such as whether the Iranian seizure decree covered foreign situated property or oil not yet extracted, or the adequacy of Mexico's promise to pay an indefinite sum in the future. All the cited examples involved

---

Holland: Rey v. Lecouturier, Sup. Ct., Mar. 3, 1908, Revue Darras 202 (1907).

Switzerland: Rey v. Jaccard, Sup. Ct., Feb. 13, 1906, Revue Darras 202 (1907); Compagnie fermière de la Grande Chartreuse v. Rey, Sup. Ct. July 17, 1913.

United States: Baglin v. Cusenier, 221 U.S. 580 (1910).

facts ostensibly bringing them within the scope of the Act of State Doctrine. But when unflinching application of the doctrine would have been to the economic detriment of the forum national, then Act of State was ignored by the court.

Some tentative conclusions can be drawn from the foregoing examples: 1) a dogmatic version of the Act of State Doctrine does not describe an international practice whereby municipal courts decline to inquire into the validity of foreign seizures of alien-owned property; 2) national courts tend ultimately to protect their own nationals from detrimental economic impact if possible, and concern themselves with legalistic features of the case in order to do that, and 3) a foreign fait accompli may be "honored" judically if the forum national has profited by it, unless there is a local impact contrary to national foreign policy vis-à-vis the seizing nation and one which the forum can effectively avoid. Foreign acts of state purporting to change the title to movables owned by aliens are freely inquired into by the courts of most nations, the foremost exception being the United States.

The following list of decided cases in addition to those already noted in this Appendix involved takings of alien-owned property by foreign states which were reviewed on the merits by municipal courts:

Austria—Dralle v. Republic of Czechoslovakia, [1950] Ann. Dig. 155

Belgium—Deville v. Servais, [1943-1945] Ann. Dig. 448

British Territories—Luther v. Sagor, (1921) 3 K.B. 532; N.V. De Bataafsche Petroleum Maatschappij v. The War Damage Commission, [1956] Int'l L. Rep. 810

Federal Republic of Germany— M. v. Aktieselskabet K.H., 145 Entscheidungen des Reichsgerichts in Zivilsachen 16 (1934), [1933-1934] Ann. Dig. (No. 217); Confiscation of Property of Sudeten Germans Case, [1948] Ann. Dig. 24, 25 (No. 12); Confiscation of German Property in Czechoslovakia Case, [1953] Int'l L. Rep. 31

France—Ropit Case, Cour de Cassation (Supreme Court) (1928), (1929) Recueil general des lois et des arrets (Sirey)

Part I, 217, 55 Journal du droit international (Clunet) 674
(1928), [1927-1928] Ann. Dig. (No. 43)

Greece—District Court of Piraeus (1937), (1937) Efimeris
Ellinon Nomicon D. 560, reported by Massouridis, "The
Effects of Confiscation, Expropriation, and Requisition by a
Foreign Authority," 3 Revue Hellenique de droit international
62, 68 (1950)

Netherlands—P.T. Escomptabank v. N.V. Assurantic Maatschappij de Nederlanden (June 6, 1963); Bank Indonesia v.
Senembah Maatschappij N.V. and De Twentsche Bank N.V.,
(1959) Nederlandse Jurisprudentie 855, portions of decisions
quoted in 7 Netherlands Int'l L. Rev. 400 (1960)

Switzerland—Rosenberg v. Fischer, [1948] Ann. Dig. 467

United Kingdom—Wolff v. Oxholm (1817) 6 M&S 92; *In re*
Helbert Wagg & Co., (1956) 1 Ch. 323, 347-49 (1956)[15]

Far from being a maxim of international judicial practice, the Act of State Doctrine (insofar as it purports to
denote exclusive and conclusive competence) is clearly the
exception and not the rule.

[15] Hearings on the Foreign Assistance Act of 1965 Before the
House Committee on Foreign Affairs, 89th Cong., 1st Sess. 594-96
(1965).

Chisholm v. Georgia, 2 Dall. 419 (1793): 75
Church v. Hubbard, 2 Cranch 187 (1804): 13 n7
CIA Mineral Yendico Rodriguez Ramos S.A. v. Bartlesville Lead & Zinc Co., 275 S.W. 388 (Tex. 1925): 28, 34
Compagnie fermière de la Grande Chartreuse v. Rey, Sup. Ct. July 17, 1913: 175
Confiscation of German Property in Czechoslovakia Case, [1953] Int'l L. Rep. 31: 176
Confiscation of Property of Sudeten Germans Case, [1948] Ann. Dig. 24, 25 (No. 12) 176
Davis & Co. v. El Aguila, W. & N.J. 1939, No. 747: 166-68
Denny, The, 127 F.2d 404 (1942): 56
Deville v. Servais, [1943-1945] Ann. Dig. 448: 176
Dix v. Bank of California National Association, 113 F.Supp. 823 (CCA 10, 1952): 29, 35
Dougherty v. Equitable Life Assur. Soc., 193 N.E. 897 (1923): 42, 45, 47, 69
Dralle v. Republic of Czechoslovakia, [1950] Ann. Dig. 155: 176
Duke of Brunswick v. King of Hanover, 2 H.L.C. 1 (1848): 9
Eastern States Petroleum Co. v. Asiatic Petroleum Corp., 28 F. Supp. 279 (U.S.D.C.S.D.N.Y., 1939): 29, 36, 166-68
Efimeris Ellinon Nomicon D. 560, District Court of Piraeus (1937), 3 Revue Hellenique de droit international 62, 68 (1950): 177
Florida, The, 133 F.2d 719 (1943): 56
Frazier v. Foreign Bondholders Protective Council, 125 N.Y.S.2d 900 (1953): 29, 34

Fred S. James & Co. v. Second Russian Ins. Corp., 146 N.E. 369 (1925): 43, 47, 48
Frenkel & Co. v. L'Urbaine Fire Ins. Co., 226 N.Y.S. 322, 167 N.E. 430 (1929): 63, 65
Glidden Co. v. Zdanok, 370 U.S. 530 (1962): 120, 122 n39
Guaranty Trust Co. v. U.S., 304 U.S. 126 (1938): 51
Harris & Co. v. Republic of Cuba, 127 S.2d 687 (1961): 29
Hatch v. Baez, 7 Hun 596 (N.Y. Sup. Ct. 1876): 23, 24, 32
Helbert Wagg & Co., In re, (1956) 1 Ch. 323, 347-49 (1956): 177
Hewitt v. Speyer, 250 Fed. 367 (1918): 28, 33
Holzer v. Deutsche Reichsbahn-Gesellschaft, 14 N.E.2d 798 (1938): 67, 69
Hudson v. Guestier, 8 U.S. (4 Cranch) 293 (1808): 13, 14, 32
James & Co. v. Russia Ins. Co., 247 N.Y. 262 (1928): 43
Joint Stock Co. v. National City Bank, 240 N.Y. 368, 148 N.E. 552, affirming 210 App. Div. 665, 206 N.Y. Supp. 476 (1925): 43, 48
Kleve v. Basler Lebens-Versicherungs-Gesellschaft, 45 N.Y.S.2d 882 (1943): 67, 69-70
Kotkas, The & The Regents, 35 F. Supp. 983 (1940): 56
Kuerschner & Rauchwarenfabrik v. N.Y. Trust Co., 126 F. Supp. 684 (U.S.D.C.S.D.N.Y., 1954): 58, 59
Latvian State Cargo & Passenger Steamship Lines v. McGrath, 188 F.2d 1000 (1951): 57
Lecouturier v. Rey, Ct. of Buenos Aires, Dec. 23, 1905, Revue Darras 612 (1907): 174
Lecouturier v. Rey (1910), A.C. 174
Lehigh Valley R. Co. v. Russin, 21 F.2d 396 (1927): 38-39

INDEX

184

186

www.ingramcontent.com/pod-product-compliance
Lightning Source LLC
Chambersburg PA
CBHW022056210326
41519CB00054B/516